"*The RCIA Journey* by Deborah M. Jones is a terrific addition to the literature now available for the catechumenate process. It is user-friendly both in style and content. Catechumens and their sponsors will find it enlightening. Returning Catholics who have been away for a long time will come to terms with the mystery of the church in a whole new way. This book is engaging, and I highly recommend it."

Rev. John Catoir, J.C.D.
Director of Evangelization
Diocese of Paterson

"I found *The RCIA Journey* by Deborah M. Jones a wonderful resource for the catechumenate stage of the RCIA process. It provides a variety of ways in which solid doctrine as well as many of our Catholic customs can be shared with catechumens and candidates. Deborah Jones makes excellent use of both small group and large group dynamics. Her prayer experiences should provide real spiritual growth among the participants. The discussion questions are both relevant and challenging, thus providing for lively interaction.

The Scripture references for all three cycles (with suggested themes for each Sunday) will be a valuable resource for all RCIA session planners.

Sr. Blanche E. Cadotte, DHS, D-Min.
RCIA Parish Team Coordinator

The
RCIA

Journey...

A Resource
for the Catechumenate

Deborah M. Jones

TWENTY-THIRD PUBLICATIONS
Mystic, CT 06355

All Scripture texts are taken from *The New Revised Standard Version*, Collins Publishers 1989 (with a few clearly indicated exceptions) and are used by permission of the publishers. Other quotations from copyrighted material are credited in the Acknowledgments page.

Previously published by
Kevin Mayhew Ltd
Rattlesden
Bury St. Edmunds
Suffolk IP30 OSZ

Twenty-Third Publications
185 Willow Street
P.O. Box 180
Mystic, CT 06355
(860) 536-2611
800-321-0411

ISBN 0-89622-741-3
Library of Congress Catalog Card Number 97-60966
Printed in the U.S.A.

Acknowledgments

The authors and publishers would like to thank the following publishers for permission to reproduce passages from the publications listed.

Ave Maria Press, Notre Dame, Indiana 46556, for the text of "The Prayer of Abandonment" by Charles de Foucauld, from *Praise Him!* edited by W.G. Storey.

Catholic Adult Education Centre, Cnr. Howard & Rosslyn Streets, West Melbourne, Australia: *Towards Adult Faith.*

Catholic Housing Aid Society, 189a Old Brompton Road, London SW5 0AN: *The Roots of Social Injustice,* by T. Cullinan.

Catholic Truth Society, 38-40 Eccleston Square, London SW1V 1PD: *Christian Love and Human Sexuality,* by Cardinal Suenens.

Geoffrey Chapman, a division of Cassell Publishers, Ltd., Artillery House, Artillery Row, London SW1P 1RT, for the text of *Christ Be Beside Me,* by James Quinn, S.J.

Collins Publishers, 8 Grafton Street, London W1X 3LA: *Hungry for God,* by R. Martin; *Our Faith Story,* by A.P. Purnell; *Jesus Christ: the Way, the Truth, the Life,* by D. Konstant.

Darton, Longman & Todd Ltd., 89 Lillie Road, London SW6 1UD: *Letters from the Desert:* by C. Carretto; *The Jerusalem Bible.*

Doubleday & Co., 1540 Broadway, New York, NY 10036, USA: *The Gospel According to St. John.* Vol 1.

Liguori Publications, Liguori, Missouri 63057, USA: *Helping Your Child to Know Right from Wrong,* by Christopher Farrell.

Liturgy Training Publications, 1800 North Hermitage Avenue, Chicago, Illinois 60622-1101, USA: *Guide for Sponsors,* by Ron Lewinski. (Copyright Archdiocese of Chicago.)

Rev. B. O'Connor, O.S.A., Austin Friars School, Carlisle, Cumbria CA3 9PB: *Celebration in Faith,* by F. O'Connor.

Paulist Press, 997 Macarthur Boulevard, Mahwah, N.J. 07430, USA: *The Book of Sacramental Basics,* by Tad Guzie.

Prayer for Peace. The Prayer for Peace, by Satish Kumar, which has no ties with any single denomination or faith, is said daily at noon in many countries throughout the world and has been translated into more than 40 languages.

S.P.C.K., Holy Trinity Church, Marylebone Road, London NW1 4DV: *Baptised into Hope,* by E. Sullivan.

Tabor Publications, a division of DLM Inc., Allen, TX 75002, USA: *Unconditional Love* by John Powell, S.J.

Contents

Introduction

One after another, parishes throughout the world are adopting the thinking and practice of the RCIA, the Rite of Christian Initiation of Adults. At once ancient and new, this Rite expresses the essential mission and purpose of the church: to draw all people to the Father through Christ Jesus the Son, in the power of the Holy Spirit.

The Second Vatican Council in 1965 called for reinstating the catechumenate process. The Latin Rite's final revision was promulgated by a decree from the Congregation for Worship on January 6, 1972. The American translation was approved by the National Conference of Catholic Bishops on November 11, 1986 and confirmed by the Congregation for Divine Worship on February 19, 1987. "From 1 September 1988 the use of the *Rite of Christian Initiation of Adults* is mandatory in the dioceses of the United States of America. From that day forward no other English version may be used" (Decree issued on March 18, 1988 by the NCCB).

New members of the church are led, by stages and at their own pace, into full participation with the community of the faithful alongside whom they have journeyed. That community develops its proper identity as an evangelizing, welcoming, faith-sustaining body.

A Time Between

There is a time between two of the liturgical rites, the Rite of Acceptance or Welcoming and the Rite of Election or Enrollment. This time, called the catechumenate period, is designated for the systematic exploration of the thinking and practice of Catholic Christianity as the nurturing and growth of the person's faith and conversion to God take place.

This book is primarily intended to help those parishes in which people are embarking on the catechumenate period of the RCIA, or those who would like a change in the materials they are using. Ideas and suggestions are given here for candidates, catechumens, and their friends and sponsors, group leaders, and other parishioners for use during this period.

This book is simply *one* resource in a process that takes into account the needs and development of each individual. The process itself has to be flexible and adaptable. No one resource could pretend to answer all questions about Catholic life and belief. The most important resource is the living witness and testimony of the many good and faithful Catholics to be found in every parish.

While this book is primarily for catechumens and their sponsors, it can also be used with candidates for full reception into the Catholic Church; returning Catholics who have been away from church for many years; the team of catechists, group leaders, and helpers; and friends and supporters of the above from the parish at large.

How to Use This Material

This book is divided into units of material for twenty sessions. These can be taken in any order. Since the RCIA is a liturgically based process, an Appendix provides the Scripture readings for each Sunday and suggested possible topics that can be effectively used with the readings. This Appendix will help decide the order in which the units are used in any particular year.

Before each session, the text for the next unit should be read at home.

Begin each session by reviewing the text of the unit, especially as some participants may not have had the opportunity to read it in advance. An important part of the reviewing process is inviting and answering questions. A copy of the *Catechism of the Catholic Church* may be useful for reference.

Next, move on to the suggestions for Large Group and Small Group work, adapting them to suit your group.

Each session concludes with a short period of prayer. This material has been designed with the needs of the average, "ordinary" parish in mind (in the hope that nobody is offended by that description!).

Three Golden Rules

It will help those in the catechumenate period, and yourselves, if you can cultivate the following three golden rules for fruitful faith-sharing groups.

1. Be a good friend: be friendly and welcoming; take the initiative in "breaking the ice"; invite the catechumen or candidate to your home for coffee or a meal; see that no one is prevented from attending because he/she needs a ride, or a babysitter; share some of the chores and projects.

2. Be a good listener: pay real attention to what others are saying, rather than focusing on your own agenda. Hogging the floor or flooding people with information can really be overwhelming.

3. Be respectful (on two levels): never try to belittle or insult another's past, background, or beliefs; and always respect the other person's doubts and difficulties. If you try to force an opinion on others, they will walk away. If they want to walk away for any reason, they must be free to do so.

So, be real, be respectful, be friendly. After all, don't *you* prefer others to be so?

A Note about Terms

We use the term Large Group when referring to all the people at a meeting. If you can divide this into even two or more groups of three to seven people, you have the Small Groups in which the personal sharing takes place. Each Small Group requires a Small Group Leader who sees to it that everyone has the opportunity to participate freely. The overall Team Leader or Coordinator, who may or may not be a priest, will need to share the responsibility for the course with a Team, to include the Small Group Leaders; those responsible for hospitality, e.g., the host/ess; those who will be Session Leaders, i.e., in charge for a Session—

Group Session

reviewing the text at the beginning of the unit for that session, timekeeping, and anything else which may need to be done to ensure that the session runs smoothly.

If possible try to see that *everyone* has a copy of this book, so that there is no mystique or "us-and-them" involved. It would also be good to have each person bring a notebook. This enables them to respond in writing and keep their responses for later reflection. It also saves having to pass out paper and pencils each time.

1. The Importance of Story

"The story that *must* be told!!!" screams the newspaper headlines. Usually though, the reality is no more than the trivial scandal of a misspent, if well-paid, life! Some stories, however, really *do* have to be told, even at the cost of torture and death for the teller.

From the first Christian martyr, St. Stephen, to those of today, exiled or imprisoned, there have been men and women in every generation who refused to be silenced. The story they told is ever the same. It centers on the life and work of one man, Jesus, the great storyteller himself.

We can hear their story today and we may run the risk of being captivated by it. We face the challenge of having our lives changed by that story and of finding ourselves compelled through sheer joy to tell that story ourselves.

It is human and right to ask questions about life and its meaning: the Greek philosopher Socrates said that the unexamined life is not worth living. Somewhere along the line, we all ask deep within ourselves: What is my life for? This is an important and sometimes painful question that must be asked if we are to grow.

Questions About Life

It is also human and right to stand in awe and wonder, or fear and rage, at the something beyond us which we sense is there: "How many men and women have looked up in fear at the thunder or the shadows in the forest and wondered about the power they sensed beyond the natural processes of the world and life?" (Ralph Martin, *Hungry for God).*

Stories take us *beyond* the world of simple facts and figures. All of the world's religions explain their deepest truths through story. Stories can *stand for* more than what can be touched and seen. The parables that Jesus told are earthly stories with heavenly meanings. Jesus did not invent this form of storytelling. He was steeped in the Old Testament tradition of using parables and allegories: the creation stories, Jonah, Job, and so many others.

Stories about Jesus

While Jesus told stories about God's kingdom being close to the poor, the ordinary, the humble of heart, others were to tell stories about him. Matthew, Mark, Luke, and John wrote their own collections of stories, which rang true to the memories of those who had heard and known Jesus. The church continues to ensure that these stories and their intended meanings remain as authentic and true today as they were when told by those who knew Jesus, the teacher from Nazareth.

At times in its history the church has been threatened by interpretations of its stories because they led to division. These were called heresies and each time such a heresy threatened, the church returned to the stories about Jesus to discern and seek out the truth, with the guidance of God's Spirit of Truth. This would then be put into the form of a statement of doctrine. The Creed, which we say together at Sunday Mass, is a collection of such statements.

Stories need discernment, and doctrine helps us to interpret stories truly. There is no opposition between stories and doctrine. In fact, tradition is made up of the stories and doctrines of the followers of Jesus throughout the years. Scripture is part of the tradition, and there is no opposition between Scripture and doctrine either.

"Stories" about God

When we talk about God in the form of statements, we can make some positive assertions:

God is all-knowing: everything is uncovered and open to the eyes of God.

God is almighty: nothing is impossible to God.

God is present everywhere: God is not bound by physical barriers, but is present to all and in all.

God is eternal: God is not bound by barriers of time, cannot be subject to aging or decay. In God's time, all is present, all is *now*.

Greek philosophy helped us to make these statements

about God. It helped us to appreciate the "otherness" of God. The Jews, the people of the Bible, so respected the otherness (or transcendence) of God that they avoided using God's name, replacing it with "The Lord" or a descriptive phrase. Being great storytellers, the Jews much preferred to describe *how* God worked, rather than making statements. They described God as a potter molding creation (Is 64:8; Jer 18:2); as a warrior defending people (Ex 15:1); as a mother, comforting her children (Is 66:13); and as a shepherd guiding his helpless sheep (Ps 23).

Our Own Stories

When we begin to share the story of our lives with others, when we open up to our brothers and sisters, we can be helped to see how God is working in our lives. To hear the story of another's life and experience is to receive a precious gift. It is to discover an unwritten page of Scripture. We may need to develop the skill of attentive listening and to pray for the discernment to be able to read God's story in another's life.

For God is not *only* the creator of worlds without end, the sublime otherness; God is also parent in all our many daily and even lifelong experiences: growing up, maturing, falling in love, getting a job, settling down, pursuing hobbies, etc. God is present in our happiness or sorrow, health or sickness, successes or failures, in a word, in every situation in our lives. God's story and the story of Jesus continues in us.

The Group Session

A word to the leaders before the Group Session starts. For this first meeting it is important to establish a warm, welcoming, friendly, confidential, open, fun, and yet worthwhile atmosphere. In as comfortable and pleasant an environment as possible (if necessary, brighten up the room with posters, flowers, etc.), see that everyone is greeted on arrival, given a cup of tea or coffee, and seated in an arrangement in which everyone can see everyone else. Music playing quietly in the background may help to break the ice.

When all are settled and relaxed, the team leader can officially welcome everybody and introduce him/herself.

The Leader should also explain how the sessions are going to operate, and check that times and dates are convenient for most people (they never will be for all!). This is also a good time to find out if anyone will need transportation, babysitters, or other practical assistance, and to put them in touch with someone who can help. Let each team member introduce him/herself, and just before breaking into groups of six to eight, have the session leader outline the theme. If participants have not yet had the opportunity to read the text for chapter one, it may be necessary to go through it in more detail than on future occasions when everyone will have read it beforehand.

Small Groups

In the Small Group, each person should briefly introduce him/herself: "I'm Mary Mills, from the new subdivision by the hospital. I'm married to Jim and have two boys, 8 and 13. I'm a housewife and an Avon lady. I've come with Jim, and know only two people here."

The next round could involve a sharing of "faith stories" and what members hope for from these sessions, e.g., "I'm not Catholic but am married to a Catholic, and I would like to know more about the Catholic faith now that the children are asking questions."

"I was baptized Catholic, but our family didn't go to church. I'd like to know what it's really about now."

"I was never baptized, but I feel a strong attraction to the Catholic church. I want to see if this is where God is calling me."

Discussion could take off from there, or may be helped by the following questions:

•Have your ideas about Catholics or Catholicism changed over the years? In what ways?

•How was the image or idea of God conveyed to you in the past? Which images have you found particularly helpful or unhelpful?

•Jesus was a great storyteller. Which of the many stories Jesus told can you remember that help you to imagine what God is like?

•Have you ever felt a real need for God in your life?

•How do you feel about the idea of God being interested and involved in every aspect of your life? Does it worry, comfort, or excite you? Can you believe it?

Allow forty minutes or so and then once again reassemble into a large group. Take any questions or comments from the small groups. Encourage everyone to read the text of the unit to be used next, before the next meeting. Conclude with a closing prayer (see following).

Closing Prayer

Invite participants to be seated comfortably, hands relaxed, eyes closed. Encourage them to say a prayer word or phrase over and over, e.g., Creator of the World, Jesus, Shepherd, Comforter, and to allow an image of God to form in their minds. Invite them to thank God for being the way God is, and for loving them.

When distractions occur, they should repeat the word they have chosen, talking naturally, addressing God with their chosen word. Encourage them to be comfortable with silence.

Allow several minutes for this and then introduce the closing prayer. Be conscious of the fact that participants may not know the traditional prayers of the church, so be sure that these are written out somewhere for them, e.g., on a poster or on a printed handout sheet. For this session, an appropriate prayer is the *Glory Be*.

Glory be to the Father,
and to the Son,
and to the Holy Spirit,
as it was in the beginning,
is now,
and ever shall be
world without end. Amen.

2. The Road to Faith

There is a view that treats faith as if it were a thing. You either have it or you don't! You can lose it if you're not careful!

This view of faith tends to see God not so much as a person, but as a Holy Being or Thing to be approached only by keeping a firm grip. Heaven help you if you ever mislay it or step out of line!

Let's change the picture and look at faith rather as a living, growing relationship with God who is *active* in our changing lives. When St. John wrote his gospel, he did not once use the *noun* "faith," but chose 98 times to use the *verb* form "to believe." Thus "to believe in" may be defined in terms of an active commitment to a person, and in particular, to Jesus. It involves much more than trust in Jesus or confidence in him: it is an acceptance of Jesus and of what he claims, and it involves the dedication to one's life to him (R.E. Brown, *The Gospel According to St. John*, Vol.I).

Our Changing Lives

In our lives as a whole, we are aware of much change and growth. We are not now as we were, not even as we were yesterday! As babies, we absorbed; but now we can reflect as well. As children, we accept stories literally; now we can see meanings and interpret. As adolescents, unsure of ourselves, we conformed with others' expectations (maybe those of our rebellious friends!); now we can dare to be different, to think for ourselves.

Now, after a period of questioning, which may have been long and challenging, we can accept ideas and meanings as our own. We can own them for ourselves. Now, too, we know how much we have to *keep* growing. It is tempting to stay in the security of the past rather than to take the risks that change might bring. Yet there can be no growth without change: to become a flower, the seed must die. Growth in faith must involve taking risks. We cannot stand still.

As St. Paul said to the Christians at Philippi (3:12–16): "I have not yet won, but I am still running the race, trying to capture the prize for which Christ Jesus captured me... I am racing for the finish...let us go forward on the road that brought us to where we are."

Progress on the road of faith does not necessarily mean knowing lots of *facts* about God. The *faith-knowledge* of God is more like that between two lovers: spending time quietly together, yearning to be with the other, and loving what the other loves.

A.P. Purnell has written, "Faith is the relationship, the incredible, tender love of God for me, and my tentative response. Beliefs describe the relationship: they attempt to put into words what faith is, so that I can share my faith with others."

All At Different Points

We are all at different points along that road of faith. Each person has a unique, individual faith-journey. But we are not expected to make the journey on our own, unaided. The whole church is a people on the move, a "pilgrim people." God is always actively with us, prompting us to help one another along the road.

When the Jews, our faith-ancestors, were enslaved in Egypt and exiled to Babylon, and when Jesus' own friends were caught up in his betrayal and execution, it seemed that misery, bondage, and despair would always be their lot. It was only after liberation from these hardships that on reflection they could see that God had been *active* in their situations, always leading them along to freedom and fullness of life.

They went from slavery in Egypt, through the desert to the promised land of freedom; from exile in Babylon to return with renewed ardor to Jerusalem. And Jesus went from crucifixion to resurrection and new life for all.

God Is Actively Involved

God is and always has been actively involved in human history, in the lives of each one of us. This follows from the very nature of God's own self. God *is* active relationship. This is expressed in terms of Trinity: three persons in the one God.

While the three persons relate to each other and to us as God's creation, God remains always one. There is only one God: one in nature, in substance, and in essence, the beginning and the end of everything. It is the one God who was revealed to Moses as "I Am" (Ex 3:14) and to the people Israel as the Lord whom they were to love "with all their heart and soul and might" (Dt 6:4–5).

"The mystery of the Most Holy Trinity is the central mystery of Christian faith and life. It is the mystery of God in himself. It is therefore the source of all the other mysteries of faith, the light that enlightens them" (*Catechism of the Catholic Church*, 234).

The one God has been revealed as Father, Son, and Holy Spirit. God the Father is always, overflowingly, loving the Son, whom he brings into being (begets) every moment. This love knows no bounds, always exceeding everything that we can think or say about it.

God the Son responds with equally constant love. Jesus of Nazareth and the Son are one and the same, although for his earthly life "he did not regard equality with God as something to be exploited, but emptied himself taking the form of a slave, being born in human likeness" (Phil 2:6–7).

God the Spirit, the "Lord, the giver of life" (*the Creed*), is the Spirit of Christ, the Spirit of God's love. This immeasurable love expressed by Father to Son, Son to Father, is eternally life-giving. Life and love are one to God who is boundless, creative energy.

The Group Session

In the large group, welcome everyone; answer questions; review the theme. Prepare several readers to read the following passages concerning the Exodus experience: Exodus 1:13–15, Exodus 6:5–8, Isaiah 41:9–15, Exodus

15:1–2; 13:17–18, Micah 6:4, 8.

Pick up and discuss any points of interest that are expressed after these readings.

In small groups, suggest these ideas for discussion topics:

•Looking back over your own faith journey, who has been the person who has most helped you along the way? Has there been more than one person?

•Has your faith journey been one of smooth, unwavering growth, or have there been ups and downs?

•How does it help you to know that we are *all* on the move and at different points in this journey?

•Have you ever experienced "exodus" in your own life? Can you see where God has been actively liberating you?

• Do you feel that you are still in bondage? In what ways?

•How would you describe what "faith" is, and what "beliefs" are?

Allow sufficient time for discussion.

When you reassemble as a large group, take any comments and questions from the small groups. Encourage everyone to spend some time at home in reading the text for the chapter you will be using next.

Closing Prayer

When all are calm and settled, read Luke 24:13–35 straight through. Then read it again *slowly*, and ask the following questions (leave a moment of silence between each question).

•After verse 14: We too have been sharing our stories; think back over the things that have been said in this session. What was most meaningful to me?

•After verse 24: The two disciples were open to the stranger. How open am I?

•After verse 27: Christ uses Scripture to throw light on his story. How can I allow Scripture to shine its light on the experiences of my life, to see God's activity in the ordinary events of my story?

•After verse 28: Christ does not force himself on others. Do I ever try to dominate or force my opinions on others? Can I let people go, or do I cling to them?

•After verse 29: Am I hospitable, generous, thoughtful, welcoming?

•After verse 32: Does my heart burn within me as the Scriptures are explained? Do I recognize my Lord, Jesus the Christ, in the "breaking of the bread"? At moments of great insight, am I aware of God's saving activity?

•After verse 35: Does reflection lead me to action? Do I find that I *have* to tell the story? *My* story? With whom shall I share my story?

Conclude by saying together the *Our Father* as in Luke's gospel (11:2–4):

Father, may your name be held holy,
may your kingdom come.
Give us each day our daily bread,
and forgive us our sins as we forgive others,
and deliver us from evil. Amen.

3. The Place of Conversion

"I was a real problem child by the time I was adopted. I'd gone through loads of foster parents, making their lives hell! When I went to live with Mom and Dad just after I was eight, I didn't think I'd be with them for long. Every time I had a screaming fit, or whatever, I'd think 'This is it! They'll send me back now, for sure.' But they never did. I can't get over how patient they were with me. Over the years I changed, of course. I tried to be nicer to them. It didn't always work, but each time I'd turn back to them and know their love would be there. I only hope that when Trev and I marry and have kids, we'll be to them like my parents have been to me."

This is Karen's story, and obviously her conversion took years. There was no "blinding flash" or instant emotional turnaround. To be a Christian means to experience conversion. Sometimes the lifelong process begins with a bang, a fundamental change of heart, or it begins almost unnoticed, from early childhood, little by little.

As A.P. Purnell says in his book, *Our Faith Story*, "We are on a journey to God: we have not reached our goal. We are in the process of becoming: we have not yet become what we are called to be."

To Be Fully Human

What *are* we called to be? We are called to be as fully *human* as was Jesus of Nazareth. He was a man who lived fully for God and for his brothers and sisters, all the world's people. He is God's answer to the question: "What is *human*?" How he is, is how God intends us to be.

Again Purnell says, "Each time I make a choice for what is more fully human, I allow God's love to touch me and I respond to life. I yield a little selfishness, see a little clearer, trust a little more, so I journey on: God's love has worked a conversion (albeit very small) in me. Conversion is all about taking little steps towards becoming more and more human, according to God's understanding of human."

Religious conversion, the Canadian theologian Bernard Lonergan explains, is the basis for all others. Through this we learn to appreciate life as "a mystery to be lived fully," a gift from God, rather than as an endless series of problems to be solved or obstacles to be overcome.

From this we learn to accept and use our emotions and feelings creatively, seeing them as a normal part of human life. Intellectually we begin to let go of knowledge as just "the facts" and see instead how knowledge can give meaning to our lives.

Finally, on the moral level, we need to be converted from making choices based either on "the law" ("I'll get it if I don't..."), or on the selfish pleasure principle. We learn how to apply the values we believe in.

God Moves Us

Conversion is not something we can boast about: "I pulled myself up by my bootstraps!" For *we* don't do the "pulling up"; God does. On hearing the challenging words of Scripture, we may be provoked into responding to the invitation to be converted more closely into Jesus' image. But it is the ongoing presence of the Spirit in us, and in the encouragement others give us, that makes it possible. When "adults who, after hearing the mystery of Christ proclaimed, consciously and freely seek the living God and enter the way of faith and conversion, it is because the Holy Spirit opens their hearts" *(RCIA Introduction,* n. 1).

Even for the disciples, who knew Jesus intimately, the path of conversion was long and rough: "Gradually the initial 'yes' that the disciples gave to Jesus deepened, was tested, failed, and succeeded, and finally, after Pentecost, ripened into wholeheartedness" (J. McKin, *Doorways to Christian Growth).*

Scripture Conversion Stories

A blind man was brought to Jesus by his friends (Mk 8:22–26). Jesus led him gently by the hand out of the village, and in a quiet place, put spittle on his eyes and laid his healing hands upon him. Not that the man saw perfectly right away; a second application was needed, and the point was made: perfect sight, full understanding, takes place in stages, gradually, just as the disciples only *gradually* came to grasp who Jesus really was.

Nicodemus, a leading intellectual in his day, argued with Jesus, prompting him to expound some of his most significant teachings (Jn 3:1–21). Nicodemus' problem was that he could not go beyond the face value of Jesus' words. He had to be patiently guided to go beyond their literal meaning. Later Nicodemus was to defend Jesus against the hostile Pharisees (Jn 7:50–51).

The Samaritan Woman (Jn 4:4–42), a woman of dubious character, belonging to a people constantly at odds with the Jews, was to become an apostle, sent to preach the Good News to her own people! Such was her remarkable conversion. Like Nicodemus, she found it difficult to interpret Jesus' words. But when at length the truth dawned on her, she had to "put down her water jar" and run to tell others. The water jar symbol of the old covenant is now replaced by the living water of the new, as it was with the wine of the new at the marriage feast at Cana (Jn 2:1–10).

The conversion of the Samaritan people also occurred by stages: first, they heard about Jesus from the woman, then they "begged him to stay with them." After two days of teaching from Jesus himself, they could *then* say: "We have heard him for ourselves, and we *know* that this is truly the savior of the world" (Jn 4:42).

Total Conversion

To be converted into the image of Jesus the Christ involves our behavior, our life-style, our attitudes, and our relationships. We need time and again, and deeper and deeper, to be liberated from our old ways and to take on newness in each area of life. The way we relate to God may need to be the first to change. We may have picked up some ideas of God that cannot be found in either Scripture or tradition, and yet which vitally affect our relationship.

For example, we may see God as an impersonal life force, or as an old bearded man on a cloud. We may see Jesus as a "superstar" or as a stern judge, sending down suffering on us as a punishment. We may see ourselves as having to merit or earn God's favor and mercy, and being generally unworthy and unlovable. We may see the church as belonging to priests and bishops, who, unlike us, are by nature holy, and so forever telling us "No, you can't!"

If we think in these ways, we are in need of conversion. We need to learn to relate to God as a fatherly, motherly, ever-loving Person; to relate to Jesus as the living risen Lord, healing now and liberating now, just as he served those he met in Palestine; to relate to the Holy Spirit as the power of the love of God, to be trusted and relied upon, rather than depending entirely on our own efforts and abilities; to relate to the church as "all of us," the whole body of believers, both those alive now and those who have gone before us, all holy, because all-loved by God.

The Group Session

In the large group welcome everyone, answer questions, and review the theme. Then ask participants to consider:

•What does Scripture tell us that we need before there can be conversion? ("A heart to understand, eyes to see, and ears to hear" [Dt 29:4]). Jesus came "so that those who do not see may see" (Jn 9:39).

• Are we being called to see something new or in a new way? Or, like the Pharisees, do we say "we see" when we don't? (Jn 9:41).

•What is God's work for us? What can we expect to happen in our lives? Do we welcome change and conversion? What might be the risks? (See Ez 36:25–28.)

•What "burning bush" experiences have we had in our lives? (See Ex 3:1–7.)

In small groups, share how at the moment when God was working through the great events of Scripture, people did not see God there. Afterwards, on reflection, they realized that God had been there, actively involved in their experience. This led them to praise and celebrate. Encourage participants to look back on their own life experiences. Can they recognize where God has been helping them to grow? They may want to discuss the following.

•How does Karen's story illustrate the theme of conversion?

•Have *you* a story to tell?

•Have any of your attitudes, views, or opinions changed over the last ten, twenty, or more years?

•What may have caused you to change your attitudes?

•What do you think it means that conversion is a life-long process?

When the large group reassembles, deal with any comments or questions from the small groups. Explain that conversion sometimes means balancing how we view God, faith, and religion. Ask participants to answer the following statements in silence.

•Is the church a community or an institution?

•Is worship a celebration or a duty?

•Is faith something "we" do or something "I" do?

•Is having authority a service or a position of power?

Suggest that all these descriptions are true to a certain extent, but at various times in our faith journey we are closer to one than the other.

Closing Prayer

When all are still and relaxed, one (good) reader should thoughtfully read this poem by Elizabeth Barrett Browning:

> Earth's crammed with Heaven,
> and every common bush afire with God;
> but only he who sees,
> takes off his shoes,
> the rest sit round it
> and pluck blackberries.

Allow a few moments of silence and then recite together this *Prayer of Abandonment* by Charles de Foucauld:

Father,
I abandon myself into your hands;
do with me what you will.
Whatever you may do, I thank you:
I am ready for all, I accept all.
Let only your will be done in me,
and in all your creatures.
I wish no more than this, O Lord.
Into your hands I commend my soul;
I offer it to you with all the love of my heart,
for I love you, Lord, and so need to give myself,
to surrender myself into your hands without reserve,
and with boundless confidence,
for you are my Father. Amen.

4. Jesus the Christ

If you ask a Christian "What do you believe in?" the answer should be "Not what, but who!"

Christians believe above all in the person of Jesus Christ. Believing *in* means giving all your trust, hope, life, and being to a person, knowing that that person means more to you than anyone or anything else can. Catholics also believe (that is, accept as truth) all that Jesus said and taught, as well as all that the church says and teaches about Jesus. Many of the sayings of Jesus are stunningly challenging.

"Just as I have loved you, you must love one another. By this love...everyone will know that you are my disciples" (Jn 13:34–35).

"If any want to become my followers, let them deny themselves and take up their cross daily and follow me. What does it profit them if they gain the whole world, but lose or forfeit themselves?" (Lk 9:23–25).

"If you forgive others their failings, your heavenly Father will forgive you yours" (Mt 6:14).

"Whoever wants to be first must be last of all and servant of all" (Mk 9:35).

"Love your enemies, do good to those who hate you...pray for those who abuse you" (Lk 6:27).

"Woe to you...[who] have neglected the weightier matters of the law: justice, mercy, faith!" (Mt 23:23).

"Do not store up for yourselves treasures on earth...for where your treasure is, there your heart will be also" (Mt 6:19–21).

Familiar and Bland

For many churchgoers, these sayings become rather too familiar and bland, and so lose their cutting edge. Some people can be turned off: those who see no need to change, whose life-styles are too comfortable to want to change (see Mk 10:22), or whose minds are closed (see Jn

6:60). Some Christians who really live these sayings find themselves the persecuted victims of oppressive regimes, for example in South America or the Far East.

Yet Jesus promised: "If you continue in my word, you are truly my disciples, and you will know the truth and the truth will make you free" (Jn 8:31–32). Jesus sets his sisters and brothers free to *live* in the fullest way. He came: "that they may have life, and have it to the full" (Jn 10:10).

With the fully lived life in mind, Christians choose not to prize too highly those values that come to an end when this life ends, values like success, power, wealth, and good looks. Real achievements to be cherished include having emptied yourself of all selfishness and having laid down your life for others. How the world would be transformed if there was real Christianity, where now so much lip-service is paid!

Look at Jesus

To know how to live this full life, Christians only have to look at the life of Jesus. Throughout the gospels there shines out the picture of a man who cared passionately for people. He healed, he taught, he served, he gave himself for them to the last drop of his blood. All people were equally deserving of his love: the despised poor, women, tax collectors, foreigners, the self-righteous, and known sinners. To help them to find health, wholeness, and joy, he showed them how to center their attention and energy, not on themselves, but on the worship of God and in the service of other human beings. By giving them his love, he could move even the hardest hearts, as in the account of his encounter with Zacchaeus, an unpopular and crooked collector of taxes for the Romans.

Have someone read Luke 19:1–10 aloud. Pause for a moment, and then ask the following:

- Is Jesus speaking to me as he did to Zacchaeus?
- How can I change my life, as Zacchaeus did his?

Of all the many titles and descriptions the church gave Jesus: Savior, Redeemer, Shepherd, Lord, the Greek word "Christ" (in Hebrew, "Messiah") is the one given special importance. It means anointed one. Anointing was associated in the Jewish world with healing and salvation. Also, priests, prophets, and kings were anointed as a sign that they were to serve God and the people in a special way, with God's Spirit giving them the power to do so.

Christ the Messiah

Throughout the long years when the Jewish people suffered under foreign rule, hope was mounting for a mighty military messiah to arise and save them from oppression. Could Jesus of Nazareth, with his extraordinary gifts and large following, be the one? Imagine how confused and disappointed many were at his resolute nonviolence, and especially by his humiliating death on a cross.

It took special God-given understanding by the disciples of Jesus to realize that in fact this agonizing death really *was* the ultimate victory, and that the forces over which this victory had been won, sin and death, were far stronger and more powerful than the mighty Roman Empire.

The whole person (not just the body) of Jesus suffered on the cross, and the whole person (not just the soul) was raised from death to life. Christ, in a glorified body, is now wholly in heaven and yet with us too in a new way. No wonder that we celebrate that passing over from death to life as the central focus of all our worship.

This passing of Jesus from death to life with God the Father was proof that death itself had been conquered once and for all. In John's gospel we are told how Jesus offers this same life-with-God to all people: "'I am the resurrection and the life. Those who believe in me, even though they die, will live, and everyone who lives and believes in me will never die. Do you believe this?' She (Martha) said to him, 'Yes, Lord, I believe that you are the Messiah, the Son of God, the one coming into the world'"

The Easter Event

(Jn 11:25–27). Martha expresses here the Christian under-standing of "Christ," that he is the one who is able to share the very life of God with all who believe in him. Even death cannot blot out this sharing in the divine life, which is eternal as God is eternal, and in which "your joy may be complete" (Jn 15:11).

The Group Session

In your large group welcome everyone, and then review the theme. Invite three or four team members to reflect briefly on prepared gospel passages, ones that provide special insights or that hold value for them.

In your small groups, ask each member to take a gospel passage, one of their choosing or one from this list: Mark 1:40–41 (a healing), Luke 5:27–32 (call of Levi), John 13:3–5; 12–15 (serving), Mark 10:17–22 (riches), John 4:5–10 (Samaritan woman), Matthew 5:3–12 (teaching), Mark 12:41–44 (widow's mite), Luke 18:9–14 (parable).

Then ask small group members to share in twos:

•Have you ever met anyone who seemed to bring you to life?

•What qualities did he or she have?

•Which values of Jesus do you personally find most difficult to live out?

Back in the large group, encourage a general discussion of the place of Jesus in our Christian lives.

Closing Prayer

When everyone is quiet, relaxed, comfortable, breathing gently, with their eyes closed, the leader can say to all: "Put yourself into the presence of our Lord, Jesus Christ. See him, hear him, praise him." Allow several minutes of silence. Then have a good reader proclaim the following:

In Thornton Wilder's play *Our Town*, a young woman dies and has the chance of re-living any one day from her past. She chooses her tenth birthday, and sees it all again with the eyes now of experience, of reflection. She cannot go through with the whole day, the experience is too much for her, and she breaks down and in a loud voice to the stage manager says: "I can't. I can't go on. It goes so fast. We don't have time to look at one another." (She breaks down, sobbing...and goes on): "I didn't realize. So all that was going on and we never noticed." After saying good-bye to all her childhood world, she adds: "Oh earth, you're too wonderful for anybody to realize you." (She looks toward the stage manager and asks abruptly, through her tears) "Do any human beings ever realize life while they have it— every, every minute?" The stage manager replies: "No...(pause), the saints and poets, maybe—they do some."

Allow a few moments of silence of these words to sink in. Then continue:

"Lord Jesus, lead us all to the fullness of life—to life which is realized every, every minute. Be with us, every, every minute. Open our eyes to the joy, the freshness, and wholeness of life—every, every minute."

Conclude with everyone saying the following prayer together.

1. Christ be beside me,
Christ be before me,
Christ be behind me,
King of my heart.
Christ be within me,
Christ be below me,
Christ be above me,
never to part.

2. Christ on my right hand,
Christ on my left hand,
Christ all around me,
shield in the strife.

Christ in my sleeping,
Christ in my sitting,
Christ in my rising,
light of my life.

3. Christ be in all hearts
thinking about me,
Christ be in all tongues
telling of me.
Christ be the vision
in eyes that see me,
in ears that hear me,
Christ ever be.
(From *St. Patrick's Breastplate*, adapted by James Quinn,
S.J.)

5. Jesus and Us

Jesus taught us to call God "Our Father." We are all the daughters and sons of God. Yet the relationship of Christ Jesus with the Father is unique: as the Christian Creed says, he is "the only Son of God" and he "came down from heaven for our salvation."

As the Word of God communicated to us in human form, Jesus is everything that God wants to show us about God's own self. For in John's gospel Jesus says, not only have "I made known to you everything I have heard from my Father" (15:15), but also: "If you know me, you will know my Father also" (14:7).

The Son of Man

"Son of Man" was a title that Jesus often used for himself, and it stresses the fact that he was human, that he had blood and bone and sinews. With a human mother, he grew up like any normal child of his time (what nonsense to say in a well-known carol, "The little Lord Jesus, no crying he makes"). Of course he felt hunger, weariness, and at times anger. But above all he felt compassion. In him we find the true picture of real humanity: he was uniquely perfect. He was radically open to all people and to the will of his Father.

A friend of mine stopped by her daughter's one morning to visit her little grandchild, and she found her daughter in tears at the table, though the baby looked well and happy. "Oh Mom," she sobbed, "have you seen the paper? And the news on the TV this morning? All that killing and violence! So much suffering and selfishness going on; what sort of a world is this in which to bring up my child?"

My friend knew what her daughter meant, and had sometimes asked herself the same question. The world can seem to be drowning in a flood of what can only be described as sin. We are all drawn into it, because we all live in the real world. The results of our sins are all around us: loneliness, despair, misery. Life really does not measure up to the dream world of the commercials. For many, it just falls apart. A sudden bereavement or a serious illness can force them to face the reality of their lives, and it can be frighteningly bleak.

There is nothing new here. Since the beginning of human life it has been the same: only the technology has changed.

We Need God

What we desperately need is something to smash through the vicious cycle of violence and counter-violence, oppression-liberation-oppression, guilt and revenge. We might try, but our own efforts rarely *last* even when they do succeed. No power less than God's, the ultimate source of all reality, can do this.

God, through Jesus Christ, has given us a brand-new start. As God alone can forgive sin, God the Son was sent to save and reconcile the whole world. The Christmas event, when God's son was born as a human baby, is linked inseparably with the Easter event, bringing together God's eternal time with our historic time. "Only when the love of God for humanity becomes an event in history, can a new beginning be made in history" (Walter Kasper in *Jesus the Christ*).

We now have a real alternative. Because this one person, Jesus, was perfectly obedient to God, totally loving, completely selfless, and utterly sinless, he, human like us, could be intimately united with God. This allows each one of us to relate to God in a new way. No longer can we think of God-up-there and us-down-here. Because we all relate to Jesus Christ as our brother, all of us can share in the relationship with the Father which he enjoys supremely. Now, too, we can relate to each other in a new way, not as strangers but as sisters and brothers.

God has taken us out of the power of darkness and created a place for us in the kingdom of the Son whom he loves, and in him we gain our freedom. (See Col 1:13–14).

We need not doubt the solidarity of Jesus with our-selves. He spoke of others *as if they were himself.* Read, for example: Acts 9:4–5 (persecuted disciples = "me"), and Matthew 25:34–46 (to the least of my brothers = to me).

"The time is fulfilled," Jesus said, "and the kingdom of God has come near; repent, and believe in the good news" (Mk 1:15).

The Kingdom of God

The Good News is that the kingdom of God, the age of love, has begun in human history through the life, death, and resurrection of Jesus Christ. It is a message of joy. All human hopes and longings can be fulfilled and a com-pletely new start be made. All the old corrupt values are reversed: it is those who mourn, who are despised, poor, persecuted; it is the "little" people who are blessed!

This is a message of life: it refers to every act of God's will freely carried out in the here and now by men and women. Every act of kindness, healing, forgiveness is a deed of both the doer and of God. God invites us to have a share in his own life and to be partners in the ongoing creation of the world.

It is a message of hope as history is still going on, and all of us are still on the journey. God's will is still in the process of being fulfilled, and so the kingdom is still com-ing. We are assured that love *will* triumph over evil in the end, as it did at a point in history on a cross outside Jerusalem, and that the kingdom of God will arrive in its fullness. For this we pray daily: "Thy kingdom come: thy will be done on earth as it is in heaven."

The Group Session

In your large group, welcome everyone, answer questions, and review the theme. It may help you to draw out points by using Titus 3:3–6. In your small groups, invite partici-pants to respond to the following statements about Jesus. As each statement is read, ask members to decide whether they would answer yes or no. After a pause, discuss the statement. Then move on to the next statement. Or go

through all the statements before starting your discussion.
Is it true that Jesus...

•was a good man, but little more than that? yes/no

•was God, just seeming to be human? yes/no

•was a circumcised Jew? yes/no

•knew everything about everything from infancy? yes/no

•was not able to sin? yes/no

•is related to all of us? yes/no

•offers us a life of pleasure? yes/no

•prefers some people to others? yes/no

•affects our lives only after death? yes/no

•performed miracles as signs that God's kingdom had come? yes/no

•rewards only those who have deserved it? yes/no

•is living, loving, and active now? yes/no

In pairs, have them consider the following: If you had to describe Jesus to a Martian, what would you choose to say about him? Write down your ideas in just one or two sentences, then tell your partner. Use words and phrases that a non-Christian can readily understand.

Back in your large group, have a general discussion about the Jesus statements. Share what Jesus means to you. If there is time, invite others to tell who Jesus is for them.

Closing Prayer

Invite everyone to sit quietly for a moment, inhaling the peace of God's presence and exhaling all that is distracting or troubling. Then invite participants to repeat after you, phrase by phrase, the *Jesus Prayer*:

Lord Jesus Christ,
Son of the Living God,
have mercy on me, a sinner.

Then, in silence, invite everyone to repeat this phrase over and over letting it sink deep into the heart, slowly, with meaning.

After five minutes or so, conclude with everyone saying this *Compline Prayer:*

Save us, Lord, while we are awake;
protect us while we sleep;
that we may keep watch with Christ
and rest with him in peace. Amen.

6. The Old Testament

"Long ago God spoke to our ancestors in many and various ways" (Heb 1:1).

Jews and Christians have much in common. The good news of God's love for all people was first revealed to the Jews, the people chosen by God for a purpose. To be a chosen people meant that they were to be a sign of God's love for all people. It was during their long history that this sign became perfected in one of their number, Jesus. Since then both Christianity and Judaism have upheld the values and cherished the revealed insights of who God is, found in the books of the Hebrew Bible (Old Testament).

Who Wrote the Old Testament?

At the deepest level, God is the author of the Scriptures. God is speaking to us through the written words of people. Those who wrote down or edited all the stories, poems, and accounts (some of which were already many hundreds of years old) naturally used their own understanding and style. Remember that people of other ages and countries use language in ways way we don't necessarily understand. For example, in the early stages of history, to show that some people led good lives and were blessed by God, their ages were highly exaggerated. Kenan lived for 905 years, and Methuselah for 969!

If you are bothered by some accounts that do not tally with the discoveries of modern science, look instead for what the author *meant* by the story. What is intended is probably a parable-story, at one level about ordinary life, but at a deeper level about God and heavenly matters. The deeper level is the important one.

Genesis, the Book of Beginnings, contains many of these parables. Through them we can learn that the creator-God made human beings in his own image, both men and women equally, and gave them free will, freely to accept or freely to reject God's love. We can see that by rejecting God's love and disobeying God's loving commands, sin with its consequences is set loose in the world. Yet God is shown as never giving up. To the obedient Noah and every living thing that is found on the earth (Gn 9:17), God offered a covenant (i.e., a relationship based on promises) marked with the sign of a rainbow.

Abraham too, our "father in faith," was offered a covenant with the promise that his people would become a great nation under God's special care. Shedding the blood of sacrificial lambs was to be offered as *an act of worship, appeal for forgiveness,* and as a means of *renewing* the nation's relationship with God.

Circumcision was required of the male population as the sign that the covenant was endorsed by the people. Abraham's grandson Jacob (also called Israel) had twelve sons who each founded a tribe which together became the nation of Israel. One of these sons, Joseph, helped the people to settle in Egypt, where they eventually became slaves of the Pharaoh, and were forced to labor in the building of the pyramids and palaces.

Three Key Moments

The first key moment of the Old Testament involves Moses leading Israel from slavery in Egypt through the Red Sea to new life. A new covenant (see Ex 19) was made between God and the people, based on the Ten Commandments and the Teaching, or Law (in Hebrew, this is known as the Torah). After Moses died, the people settled in Canaan (which the Romans later called Palestine after the Philistine people). They became first farmers, then town-dwelling crafts- and tradespeople.

Tribal organization tends to break down when people begin to live in towns. Old loyalties give way to new, and people need to find security and pride in different social structures. For the Jewish people at that time, the sense of being part of a united and great nation was given popular expression with the appointment of the first national king, Saul.

A second key moment was the appointment of David as the second king. He proved to be a brilliant politician, and he established Jerusalem as the military and political center of a powerful nation. He built the first temple, later made more magnificent by his son, Solomon, and it became the center of all religious life and worship. After Solomon, the kingdom split into two rival kingdoms: North (Israel), and South (Judah), (from which comes the word "Jew"). Mighty empires were rising in the East. First Assyria swallowed up Israel in 722, and then the Babylonian Empire took Judah, forcing many of her inhabitants into exile in Babylon in 586 B.C.

A third key moment was the exile. During these painful years, urged by prophets, a "remnant" of the people stayed faithful to God and the Torah, and they began to hope for a messiah to restore to them the glory of David's reign. They did eventually return to Israel and they rebuilt the devastated temple, but they were ruled over by foreign powers: Persian, then Greek, and finally Roman. The Romans destroyed Jerusalem in A.D. 70 and scattered the Jewish people throughout the world. Since then, whether in Spain, Eastern Europe, the United States or, since 1948, in Israel again, many of the Jews have kept and developed their deep faith in the one God and still observe many of their ancient traditions.

The Hebrew Bible

The Hebrew Bible was divided by the Jews into three sections: 1) Teaching (Torah), 2) the Prophets, and 3) the Writings.

Genesis, Exodus, Leviticus, Numbers, and Deuteronomy are the teaching books. The whole Bible teaches about God, of course, but these first five books (attributed to Moses) are especially sacred. They contain pre-history parable-stories, the origins of Jewish history and religion, and the rules for establishing a God-centered society.

The earlier prophets are Joshua, Judges, Samuel (I & II), Kings (I & II). The later prophets are Isaiah, Jeremiah,

Ezekiel, and the Twelve (Hosea, Joel, Amos, Obadiah, Jonah, Micah, Nahum, Habakkuk, Zephaniah, Haggai, Zechariah, Malachi).

Christians classify some of these as books of history, whereas in Jewish tradition emphasis is put on their prophetic value (speaking of God's truth to people of all times).

The task of the prophets is to call the people back to true religion. "What does the Lord require of you but to do justice, and to love kindness, and to walk humbly with your God?" (Micah 6:8).

Through them, God reveals the promise of the age of Christ (messianic era) expressed with stunningly poetic beauty in Isaiah 40–55 (highly recommended reading!).

The Writings are Psalms, Job, Proverbs, Ruth, Song of Songs, Ecclesiastes, Lamentations, Esther, Daniel, Ezra, Nehemiah, and Chronicles. These books involve the response of people to God's revelation, particularly in the teaching.

The Greek Bible

This is a Greek translation of all the Hebrew books above, plus seven later books written in Greek: Tobit, Judith, Maccabees I & II, Wisdom, Ecclesiasticus, Baruch, and parts of Esther and Daniel.

All forty-six of these were in use by and accepted by the Christian church in the year A.D. 100. They have continued to be the books of the Catholic and Orthodox Bibles. The sixteenth-century reformers accepted only the thirty-nine Hebrew books. Now, however, through joint Bibles and Bible study, many accept and value those books once called Apocrypha (hidden). In the early days of the church, there were many apocryphal books in circulation, but the church was guided by the Holy Spirit to select only those that are sound in teaching and true in revelation.

For hundreds of years, stories, songs, and prayers were passed on by word of mouth. It is not easy to date when they *started* to be written down, certainly not before reading and writing had begun to be more widespread, about 900 B.C., with most books being written or assembled over several centuries. The Torah was finished and accepted by 400 B.C. and the Prophets by the second century B.C. The youngest of all the books, Wisdom, was probably complete by 50 B.C.

The Group Session

With your large group, welcome everyone, answer questions, and review the theme. It may be necessary to expand on concepts like covenant and Torah or symbolic versus literal language.

Three or four team members might want to share a passage from the Old Testament that they consider significant. Any impression that the God of the Old Testament is vengeful or savage, unloving or remote should be discussed and corrected.

In the small groups, members might share their own favorite passage, or spend three or four minutes on each of the following:

Ezekiel 37:21–28 (promise of the age of the messiah), Isaiah 55:3–9 (promise of a new covenant), Deuteronomy 24:14–22 (justice), Isaiah 61:1–2 (good news; see also Luke 4:18), Joel 2:12–13 (call to real repentance), Psalm 89:1–4 (hymn to God's faithfulness), Isaiah 49:13–16 (God never abandons us), Exodus 19:3–8 (obedience demanded and accepted).

Back in the large group, deal with any comments or questions from the small groups. Invite people to share what seemed to them insightful or helpful, and then create a prayerful atmosphere by allowing a few moments for silent reflection.

Closing Prayer

Invite members to look at Psalm 27 (Yahweh is my light and my salvation) in the Jerusalem Bible version, if possible. If everyone does not have a copy, have it read aloud, slowly and carefully. Then ask members to ponder the phrases that seem most relevant to their own lives and faith-stories.

Conclude with everyone saying together the *Prayer of St. Francis:*

> Lord, make me an instrument of your peace:
> where there is hatred, let me sow love;
> where there is injury, pardon;
> where there is doubt, faith;
> where there is despair, hope;
> where there is darkness, light;
> and where there is sadness, joy.
>
> O Divine Master,
> grant that I may not so much seek
> to be consoled as to console,
> to be understood as to understand,
> to be loved as to love.
>
> For it is in giving that we receive;
> it is in pardoning that we are pardoned,
> and it is in dying that we are born to
> eternal life.

7. The New Testament

It is said that whenever St. Francis of Assisi found a scrap of paper lying beside the road, he would lift it carefully and bear it away with great reverence, just in case words of God from the Bible were written on it.

What a shock he would have in today's world! We are bombarded daily by words of all sorts, written and spoken, processed and programmed! How hard it is for us to recognize the few that give life from all the rest.

As the fourth-century Bible scholar, St. Jerome, wrote to Paula, a Roman lady who had learned the whole Bible by heart, "What food, what honey could be sweeter than... to look into the mind of the creator, to listen to the Lord's words?"

And in his encyclical, Pope Benedict wrote: "My one desire for all the church's children [is] that, being saturated with the Bible, they may arrive at that all-surpassing knowledge of Jesus Christ."

Food for the Soul

More recently in the *Decree on Revelation*, the bishops noted that the force and the power in the Word of God is so great that it remains the support and energy of the church, the strength of faith for her sons and daughters, food for the soul, and the pure and perennial source of spiritual life.

Jesus himself is the Word made flesh (see Jn 1). God speaks to us in him, through his life and his words. "...your words became to me a joy and the delight of my heart."

God is revealed through all the words of Scripture. The words themselves may not at first convey much to us. We all need help to discover in them fully the good news that the authors intended. Like the chief treasurer of Ethiopia in the account in Acts 8:26–40, when asked if he understood the prophet Isaiah whom he was reading, we, too, can answer:

"How can I unless I have someone to guide me?"

Over the centuries there have been very many Christians, especially of the reformed traditions, who have felt themselves to be individually guided by the Holy Spirit alone. Their great practice of reading the Bible privately has been of enormous help in nurturing and sustaining the faith of generations. Yet individual guidance needs to be tested with the mind of Christ, and who can guide with the mind of Christ if not the body of Christ, the church? (See chapter 8, "The Holy Spirit and the Church," for a fuller explanation of the "Body of Christ.")

The disciples on the road to Emmaus felt their "hearts burning within" them as the risen Christ explained the Scriptures to them (Lk 24:32). The chief Ethiopian treasurer was converted and baptized after Philip, starting from a Bible text, explained the good news of Jesus to him. Even today lives are changed when people hear the good news authentically presented to them.

Scripture in Church

At the celebration of every Mass, the church proclaims the Word of God in readings, teachings (homily), and prayers. Indeed Scripture (liturgy of the Word) has always been venerated by the church which has considered the liturgy of the Word and the Liturgy of the Eucharist to form together one single act of worship. "The church has always venerated the divine Scriptures as it has venerated the Body of the Lord, in that it never ceases, above all in the sacred liturgy, to partake of the bread of life and to offer it to the faithful from the one table of the Word of God and the body of Christ" (*Decree on Revelation*, n. 21).

It is good to read in advance the portions of Scripture that will be used at Mass, and to listen attentively when they are read, for "Christ himself is present in his word since it is he himself who speaks when the holy Scriptures are read in church" (*Constitution on the Liturgy*, n. 7). "To ignore Scripture is to ignore Christ" (Pope Benedict XV).

How do we read or hear the Word of God? First of all,

with prayer, with an attentive, prayerful attitude, like that of young Samuel in the temple; "Speak, Lord, your servant is listening" (1 Sm 3:10).

We should also reflect on it: considering how our own life or experience is being addressed by these words.

Finally, we read or listen with a view to action. If action does not follow, we are simply being entertained. "They hear the Word, hold it fast in an honest and good heart, and bear fruit with patient endurance" (Lk 8:15).

What Is the Source?

The books of the Old Testament, which were the Scriptures for Jesus and the early church, contained much that had been used for worship before being written and collected. In the same way material that made up the New Testament was preached, taught, and believed by the people of God before any of it was collected together as Scripture. There was much more written than what was finally selected, but the church included as holy Scripture only what it considered authentic.

First there is Jesus preaching the good news (gospel) of the kingdom of God. All that Jesus says and does is gospel, all that he passes on to his apostles or special envoys.

Then there are the apostles, the first bishops of the church, "every day in the temple and at home they did not cease to teach and proclaim Jesus as the Messiah" (Acts 5:42). Through these people and their descendants, the church grew, with new communities springing up throughout the Eastern Mediterranean.

Finally, writing was necessary to send letters off to the new communities to follow up infrequent visits. Thirteen of these by St. Paul, and eight others, are found in the New Testament. The first one, to the new group of Christians at Thessalonika, was probably written more than 20 years after Jesus told his followers to "Go, make disciples of all the nations" (Mt 28:19).

While the apostles were still living, with their memories fresh, it was enough to convey the gospel by speech. But the time arrived when it became necessary to write down accounts of "everything that Jesus had done and taught" (Acts 1:1), although really there were "many other things Jesus did; if every one of them were written down, I suppose that the world itself could not contain the books that would be written" (Jn 21:25). So, the writers had to edit and select, to choose those sayings and anecdotes of Jesus from the current collections, and, under the inspiration of the Holy Spirit, to set down their accounts to reflect the church's teaching and to meet the religious needs of their intended audience.

They Wrote the Truth

None of the four writers, or evangelists (messengers of good news) intended to write a simple biography of Jesus, nor did they know that their versions of the gospel would one day be included in Scripture. They just wrote the truth, as they and their community believed, in their own words, and for one purpose: "so that you may come to believe that Jesus is the messiah, the Son of God, and that through believing you may have life in his name" (Jn 20:31).

Tradition has passed down to us the names and backgrounds of the evangelists and the sequence of the gospels, but none of these claims is established definitively. Scholars are constantly in the process of shedding new light on these matters and discovering fresh insights into the communities of early Christians which produced these gospels.

St. Mark, possibly St. Peter's secretary and interpreter, wrote after St. Peter's death (about A.D. 65) to encourage the persecuted Christians in the Rome of Nero.

St. Matthew, one of the twelve apostles, wrote for Jews and Jewish Christians after the destruction of Jerusalem in A.D. 70. He emphasized the Messiah, the new Moses. Even in his first sentence, he links Jesus with both David and Abraham, key figures of Jewish faith.

St. Luke, like Matthew, used a lot of material from Mark's version. Luke was a Greek-speaking Gentile, and possibly secretary to Paul. He wanted all people to believe in Jesus. In his version of Jesus' family tree, he links Jesus with both David and Adam.

St. John's version of the good news was written possibly as late as A.D. 100 or so. This version is strikingly different from the other three, based as it is on teaching illustrated by seven "signs" (miracles), and prayers, speeches, and deeds of Jesus not mentioned in the other gospels. Jesus is seen here strongly representing the fulfillment of the Law, Old Testament prophecy, and the themes of the Festivals.

Links with the Old Testament

Much New Testament literature reflects the Christian interpretation of the Old Testament. One early Christian tradition viewed various Old Testament people and events as types, or foreshadowings of those in the New who are their counterparts. Jesus is seen in very many ways as fulfilling Old Testament "types."

Consider Jesus as the new and perfect Adam, making up for Adam's disobedience by perfect obedience; as the new Moses, leading us to the promised land of eternal life; as the new David, as messiah-king whose rule is perfect love; as the suffering servant in the book of Isaiah: "through his wounds we are healed" (Is 53:5); as the new temple, "destroy this temple and in three days I will raise it up" (Jn 2:19), through whom is perfect worship "in spirit and in truth" (Jn 4:23), and who is both priest and victim.

The Group Session

In your large group, welcome everyone and answer questions. Give instructions for the small group session which will follow.

Each group is to compose a short account of the good news, selecting and molding the material appropriately, so that it makes sense to, and influences, one of these:

- a highly religious non-Christian group;
- a bored, uncaring teenage group;
- a group of young children;

•a group of torturers and death-squad "hit men";

•any other?

In the small groups, have participants select a "target audience," and then spend ten minutes discussing their ideas; allow five minutes for someone to write down the account, and five minutes for completing it. Then all should return to the large group where one member from each small group can read the results of their labors. Then everyone can discuss the accounts and compare them with the gospels.

Move then into a discussion of recent readings at Mass. What stood out as memorable, striking, puzzling, challenging, etc.? Invite one or two readers to share how they prepare each reading, and what structures there are in the lectionary.

Display materials that give insights into the readings, such as *Exploring the Sunday Readings, The Word of the Lord,* and *Bringing the Word to Life* (see suggested resources at the back of this book). Show Bible commentaries, such as *The New Jerome Biblical Commentary* and versions of Bibles that contain good notes. Answer or note questions and deal with any practical matters before moving into prayer.

Closing Prayer

Invite participants to read quietly (or have someone read to them) Philippians 2:1–11. Encourage everyone to allow the words to speak directly to them. After the reading, allow a few minutes for silent prayer.

Conclude with everyone saying this prayer of St. Richard of Chichester:

Thank you, Lord Jesus Christ, for all the benefits and blessings that you have given me; for all the pains and insults that you have borne for me. Merciful Friend, Brother and Redeemer, may I know you more clearly, love you more dearly, and follow you more nearly, day by day. Amen.

8. The Holy Spirit and the Church

"No man is an island." We readily concur with John Donne. We know how dependent we are on others: for food, fuel, clothes, language, knowledge, and so much more. We were created for relationships, for belonging, for giving. We may be most aware of this through the pain of broken relationships or loneliness. The perfect relationship of love is that of the "private life" of God, in whose image we were created, the family of the Trinity: Father, Son, and Holy Spirit. Such love as theirs, so limitless and generous, is available for all to share.

For when Jesus was about to leave his disciples, he promised them that he would not leave them orphans, but would send the Paraclete (helper), the Holy Spirit, to be with them forever. Jesus had to leave the confines of time and space (first-century Palestine) in order to be with all people everywhere. In the Spirit, Jesus is no less present to contemporary disciples than he was to those with whom he walked beside the lake of Galilee.

This same creator-Spirit who had formed the world and the human race (see Genesis chapter one) was to form a new creation: a people from every race, class, and age, united in faith and love, to work as partners with the Christ, who had been sent "not to condemn the world, but in order that the world might be saved through him" (Jn 3:17).

The Spirit came (and how!) to the apostles, Jesus' mother, and other men and women followers on the festival of Pentecost, as recorded in Acts 2. From among the first chosen people of Israel, this handful of disciples formed the beginning of a catholic (worldwide) church that was to proclaim the good news of Christ Jesus across the centuries. On that Pentecost, the prophecy of Joel had begun to be fulfilled: "It is the Lord who speaks…I will pour out my Spirit upon all flesh...(and) everyone who calls on the name of the Lord will be saved" (Acts 2:17, 21).

The Spirit is poured out freely on all, enabling people to resist the pressures of selfishness and sin, and to move toward the light of truth. At baptism, this gift is celebrated and accepted. This is the first step to full participation in the Christian church and it starts a new life lived in relationship with other Christians.

Through the church's tradition—the handing down through history of the Word of God and the sacraments—we not only learn of and worship God, but also actually encounter God in many real and intimate ways. In the eucharist particularly, each participant is in the closest possible union with both God and other Christians. The community is then *fully* "the church."

The church is the context within which each of its members continues to fulfill God's work of creation and salvation.

Names for the Church

The church is sometimes referred to as "people of the new covenant." Jeremiah was promised (31:31, 33) that one day God "will make a new covenant with the house of Israel...I will put my law within them, and I will write it on their hearts; and I will be their God and they shall be my people." This was sealed on behalf of both God and people by the blood Jesus shed on the cross, to which he referred during his Last Supper (see Lk 22:20).

The church is also called the body of Christ. Through the Spirit, Christ unites his followers into a living body, his body, with Christ as the head. As all the parts of a human body together form one body, so each member of the church, with her or his special gifts and talents given by the Spirit, is united to the body of Christ, the church.

The church is the meeting-place of God and people. It is in the church that people can fully be what they are intended to be: in touch with the world and in touch with God; reaching out to others, reaching up to heaven.

Maximus the Confessor has written: "The church is the center upon which all lives converge, in order that the creatures of the one God may not live as strangers or enemies one with another, having no place in common, where they may display their love and their peace."

The Church and the World

The church is not a group of "holier-than-thou" people set apart from the world. All Christians are very much *in* the world and *for* the world, and yet, for Christians there is more to life than just the values, goals, and achievements *of* this world. They are responding to the truly human need to reach beyond; they live in the knowledge that death is not the end of everything. Their lives are constantly unsettled by the probing challenge of the gospel, yet their happiness lies precisely in following that demanding call to walk in the steps of Christ.

That is why, until the whole world shares this lasting happiness, the Christian church is a pilgrim church. It is like a group of travelers in a desert searching for living water, and for most it is a journey of hope and expectation. During the journey Christians are called to help to bring life to that desert, the world. The church, as the living body of Christ in the world, has been entrusted with the world.

St. Teresa of Avila once wrote: "Christ has no body now on earth but yours; no hands but yours; no feet but yours; yours are the eyes through which Christ looks with compassion on the world; yours are the feet through which he is to go about doing good; yours are the hands with which he is to bless people now."

Entrusting the world to human beings, even with the help of the Spirit and the church, was certainly a risk for Christ to take. We all know, painfully, the gap there is between what we are and what we should be. Even the story of the church itself (see chapter 9) is not without its horrors and failings. We do not have to be in a parish long to be aware of many causes for grumbling and complaints! Yet, despite all the faults, the sins within us and in the church and the world, Christ entrusts the world to us still.

So far, one Christian church has been mentioned, formed by Christ through the Holy Spirit by means of the apostles: they who had heard the Good News from Jesus himself, spread it, and passed it on, sharing their mission with others. Within a short time missionaries were being sent out from the twin Imperial centers of Constantinople and Rome. Those from Constantinople had developed their own patterns of prayer and eucharist, and their particular customs, including their own date for Easter. Some of the churches they founded broke with the church of Rome in the eleventh century. These are called the Orthodox churches. A small number have since returned to full communion with the bishop of Rome, the pope.

The Catholic church includes those of the Roman (Latin or Western) Rite, as well as about a dozen Oriental Rites (e.g. Byzantine, Coptic, Maronite, Ukrainian, etc.).

From one point of view the Roman Rite (Roman Catholic) church can be seen as a federation of local area churches whose bishops are in full communion with each other and with the bishop of Rome. From another, it is perceived very much as a single unit.

Christians in the West were divided at the time of the Reformation (sixteenth century), and while a large number continued in the Catholic church, many others could not accept the whole tradition of Scripture, faith, and sacraments in the forms in which the Catholic church handed them down. These broke away to form the Protestant or Reformed churches, which developed their own traditions according to the different emphases of their founders or leading members. Rather different in origin is the Anglican communion, whose varied practices and wide range of doctrinal positions help it to span the gap between the Reformed and the Catholic traditions.

*Divided
Yet One*

The (Catholic) church knows that she is joined in many ways to the baptized who are honored with the name of Christian, but who do not profess the Catholic faith in its entirety or have not preserved unity or communion under the successor of (St.) Peter (the pope). "These Christians are indeed in some real way joined to us in the Holy Spirit for, by his gifts and graces, his sanctifying power is also active in them" (*Constitution on The Church*, n. 15).

To unite all the Christian churches into one undivided communion is the urgent desire of many of Christ's followers from all traditions, so that the prayer of Jesus may be fulfilled: "that they may be one, as we are one, I in them and you (Father) in me, that they may become completely one, so that the world may know that you have sent me and have loved them even as you have loved me" (Jn 17:22–23).

The Place of Mary

Catholics have always held Jesus' mother, Mary, in high esteem, honoring her with a number of titles, particularly Our Lady and Blessed Virgin. She is remembered affectionately as the one who, with her husband Joseph, provided the child Jesus with a human model of love and wisdom, steeped as she was in the pious traditions of her Jewish heritage. She was present at Jesus' first public miracle, at the wedding feast at Cana, and at her son's cruel death. She was prominent at the descent of the Holy Spirit on the apostles at Pentecost, and Catholics believe that she is still close to her son in heaven, joining and strengthening our prayers with her own.

The reasons for the preeminence of Mary in the church are many. Her response to the angel Gabriel when the Word of God was announced to her has become a model for all Christians. She not only heard the Word—and was the first to hear the gospel (or good news) concerning Jesus, the Son of God and inheritor of God's promises to David (Lk 1:32–33), she also accepted it in faith and acted upon it. She went at once to share the good news with another, her cousin Elizabeth. Hearing, accepting, and acting on the Word of God is the mark of the true disciple as Jesus shows in Luke 8:4–21. Here the parable of the sower is illustrated by the example of Jesus' mother and brothers (close relatives) as those who "hear the Word of God and put it into practice."

In Mary's praise of God, the Magnificat (recorded in Lk 1:46–55), she both accepts and proclaims the gospel, representing in herself the honor God gives to those who are powerless and weak in the world's eyes.

When Jesus was dying on the cross, John's gospel reports that he offered the "beloved disciple," John, to Mary as a son, and told her to be a mother to John. The term used, "woman" suggests something deeper than is apparent: that Mary, the new Eve (woman) was to be the spiritual mother of the whole church, represented by John. Whenever Mary is remembered and invoked, God's generosity and graciousness are brought to mind. The influence of Mary on people "does not hinder in any way the immediate union of the faithful with Christ but on the contrary fosters it" (*Constitution on The Church*, n. 60).

The Group Session

In your large group, welcome everyone and answer questions. Explore the theme of Pentecost, especially the way in which the apostles went from fear to bold proclamation of the gospel. Discuss the effect of the Holy Spirit on the people in Scripture and in the church. Encourage personal testimony by members of the parish, prayer groups, etc.

Discuss which of many of the models of the church are most helpful, for example: Divine Institution, Pilgrim People, Barque of Peter, Vine, Servant of God, Body of Christ, Sheepfold, Rock, any others?

In your small groups, suggest these topics for discussion:

•What are your most vivid experiences of church?

•How do you feel on entering a church? Does it matter what the church is, or what it is like?

•How can we make our church more welcoming?

•Have you ever experienced a personal Pentecost?

Back in the large group, deal with any questions or comments from the small groups. After any practical matters have been discussed, begin the closing prayer.

Closing Prayer

Begin by reciting the following tradition prayer of the church in a quiet voice.

> Come, Holy Spirit, fill the hearts of your faithful,
> And kindle in them the fire of your love.
> Send forth your Spirit,
> and they shall be created.
> And you shall renew the face of the earth.

Then invite everyone to open their hearts, in silence, to receive the Holy Spirit. Say: "May our minds be receptive to God's power. Open your mind to this possibility by repeating the words 'Come Holy Spirit' to yourself over and over. Then sit quietly with these words."

After a suitable period of silence, conclude with everyone saying together:

> Holy Spirit of God,
> sent by the Father and the Son,
> fill our hearts with your love.
> Lead us to know ourselves,
> to root out our selfishness,
> and to share with others the fruits of your presence:
> love, joy, peace, patience, kindness,
> goodness, trustfulness, gentleness, and self-control.
> Amen.

9. The Church's Story

The Christian church, born at Pentecost, began with Jewish people who accepted Jesus as the messiah continuing with their traditional faith and worship—in synagogues and the temple. But they also met in each other's homes to celebrate the breaking of bread (the eucharist) as at Jesus' Last Supper. Christian worship today (prayers, blessings, gestures) still reflects these Jewish roots.

However, those Christians (first so-called in Antioch, see Acts 11:26) were thought to be heretics (holding unacceptable beliefs) by those who were not Christian. By A.D. 85 Christians were no longer welcomed in synagogues. By this time though, the Christian community had had to cope with the problem of Gentile converts. Was it necessary to become Jewish before becoming Christian, or was baptism alone sufficient? This thorny problem was resolved at the first council, when the church leaders gathered in Jerusalem in A.D. 45 (read this in Acts 15:1–35). Jerusalem's first Bishop, James, passed a ruling which enabled the church to spread throughout the Gentile world without obliging converts to become Jews first.

Growth and Risks

The church quickly spread within the Roman Empire, particularly through the tireless missionary efforts of St. Paul. Through his letters and other New Testament books, we can glimpse life as it was for those early Christians. We see that they celebrated the eucharist with words we still use today (1 Cor 11:23–26). They "were of one heart and soul, and no one claimed private ownership of any possessions, but everything they owned was held in common" (Acts 4:32). They collected money for other churches in need (2 Cor 8 and 9). They baptized all those who were prepared to risk everything, even their lives, to join them as members of the church. Indeed, hundreds were to die as martyrs (witnesses) for refusing to worship the Roman Emperor as a god.

To survive and to be effective in spreading the good news, the need for organization was soon felt. Each baptized member had to take responsibility in some way for the good of the whole group. To lead the group was a bishop, who had been taught or ordained by an apostle. When the group grew and formed new branches as time went on, priests were put in charge of them, standing in for the bishop.

The roles of bishops and priests gradually developed to adapt to changing circumstances. A particular change occurred when many monks became ordained as priests in the great monasteries that spread throughout Europe in the Middle Ages. But, to return to the earliest days of the church, deacons would help the bishop during the liturgy and women, too, helped with the baptisms and in distributing the gifts provided for the needy (1 Tim 3:8–13).

Many other orders and ministries were developed: elders, widows, gatekeepers, catechists (those who teach by sharing their faith), sponsors, readers—and whatever else was necessary. Some of these survive today, while others are being rediscovered or adapted. (See chapter 16 for more details.)

Storms and Freedom

The Christian church rode the storms of bitter persecutions, and by the year A.D. 300 was found in all parts of the Roman world. Shortly after this date, following the last and worst persecution (under Emperor Diocletian), two events occurred that rocked the world.

In A.D. 314, two years after the Edict of Toleration, which banned persecution of Christians, came the momentous Edict of Milan, in which the emperors of both East and West granted religious freedom to the church. The Western emperor, Constantine the Great, not only became Christian himself, but prepared the way for a later emperor (Theodosius) to make Christianity the official religion of the empire.

By the end of the sixth century, Christianity was firmly established as far west as Ireland, and had spread to

Southern India, Ethiopia, and even Central China. Whole peoples and armies were turning to Christianity by choice or force. And there lay the trouble.

While small communities of highly committed people could ensure strict control over important matters of faith and behavior, large numbers of reluctant or superficial Christians could easily be led astray. At times there was real confusion about what the church believed. Many people were drawn to teachings which were not the same as those preached by the apostles.

Heresies and Councils

Great numbers, for example, followed the heresy of Arius, who maintained that Jesus was not truly God, but inferior to God. Nestorius, Bishop of Constantinople, taught incorrectly that there were two persons in Christ, a divine and a human, so that Mary could be called Mother of Christ but not Mother of God!

Yet others were misled by Docetism, the idea that Jesus was really God, but only *seemed* to be human, and so could not suffer pain or have other human feelings. As the dangerous confusions arose, the church leaders met together as they had done in Jerusalem in A.D. 45 and dealt with them through a series of councils under the leadership of the bishop of Rome, successor to the apostle Peter. The conclusions of the councils are accepted as having the authority of the Holy Spirit's guidance, and so are infallible (incapable of being wrong). Some of these conclusions were in the form of creeds, statements to be recited by Christians to express their true beliefs. The one produced by the Council of Nicaea in A.D. 325, which dealt with the heresy of Arius, is the one said or sung at every Sunday Mass to this day.

Nestorius' views were countered by the Council of Ephesus in A.D. 431, which taught that Christ is a single person with two natures: human and divine. Mary is the mother of Jesus; therefore she is the mother of God.

The following council, held in Chalcedon in A.D. 451,

took on the Docetists by insisting that Christ was truly human as well as being God. Not only would the church encourage devotion to the holiness of Christ present in the eucharist, but also would stress the real human sufferings felt by Jesus at his crucifixion, through certain forms of prayer (e.g., stations of the cross, the rosary, and so on) and art. Realistic figures depicting the tortured Jesus on the cross were, and are, widespread reminders that the Son really and physically suffered for love of us.

Saints and Sinners

Councils are not the only means for keeping the Christian religion true to the Spirit of its founder. There have been times (quite a few!) when scandals and divisions, corruption and cruelty, ignorance and indifference scarred the face of the church. Yet in the darkest times, the motherly Spirit has brought forth countless saints and scholars, reformers and simple people whose influence for good would bring the Christian people back to true worship and belief.

Church Leaders Today

The word "pope" (from the Latin for "papa," as small children would call their father) was used till the sixth century to describe all bishops. It was eventually reserved for the bishop of Rome, as head of the universal church.

The bishop, who is the leading "shepherd-priest" of the local area, has as his main job to preach and teach the gospel, and to care for the priests and people within his diocese (area). He does all that a priest can do, and he also ordains priests, and confers confirmation. He often consults with groups of priests and laypeople, visits parishes, commissions people to a variety of ministries, and meets with his brother-bishop, the pope, every five years. He discusses issues with the other bishops of his country at twice-yearly national conferences. He may be sent as a representative to international synods. If a council is called, he will take part. Together the world's bishops form a college of equal partners in communion with the pope, and are to the church today what the apostles were in their time.

A dean is appointed to take certain responsibilities in looking after groups of parishes in an area *within* the diocese (called a deanery). A diocese can be broken down into many deaneries or administrative units.

In this church of Christ the Roman "pontiff" (which means bridge-builder) is the successor of Peter, to whom Christ entrusted the feeding of his sheep and lambs. Hence by divine institution he enjoys supreme, full, immediate, and universal authority over the care of souls. Since he is pastor of all the faithful, his mission is to provide for the common good of the universal church and for the good of the individual churches *(Decree on the Bishops' Pastoral Office in the Church*, n. 2).

A Modern Council

In 1959, Pope John XXIII announced that he would call together the twenty-first ecumenical council of the church, which is called the Second Vatican Council. Bishops from every part of the world and their theological advisers, observers from other churches, and a few laypeople attended the four sessions of the council from 1962 to 1965, which aimed at making decisions to renew the church.

Pope John died in 1963 and was succeeded after the first session by Pope Paul VI who continued the council in the same spirit as Pope John. By the end of the council, sixteen documents had been produced. The most important were the four constitutions: *Sacred Liturgy, Divine Revelation, The Church,* and *The Church in the Modern World.*

"In its pilgrimage on earth, Christ summons the church to continual reformation, of which it is always in need, in so far as it is an institution of human beings here on earth" *(Decree on Ecumenism*, n. 6).

The Group Session

Beforehand, contact several people from your parish who have leadership roles, and invite them to attend this meeting. See instructions below.

In your large group, invite participants to pair up and spend ten minutes brainstorming one of these statements:

•everything they know about the twelve apostles and what specific instructions Jesus gave them;

•everything they know about one of the saints, and particularly why he or she was holy.

After this brainstorming have participants move into small groups to discuss these questions:

•How are the Lord's instructions carried out now?

•How are major questions settled today?

•How does authority work now?

•How is the Lord made present here and now?

Back in the large group, introduce your guest speakers and invite them to describe their roles briefly, taking questions. They may want to relate their present ministry to ministries in the early church.

Closing Prayer

When all are settled, have five readers each take a section from Isaiah 55. (It is important that there be substantial pauses between each reading.) Voice 1: verses 1–2; Voice 2: verses 3–5; Voice 3: verses 6–9; Voice 4: verses 10–11; Voice 5: verses 12–13.

Allow for a period of silence after the reading for all to make personal connections. Conclude with everyone saying the following prayer together:

Lord Jesus Christ, Son of the living God, teach us to walk in your Way more trustfully, to accept your Truth more faithfully, and to share your Life more lovingly. By the power of the Holy Spirit, help us in our work for the church so that we may come as one family to the kingdom of the Father, where you live for ever and ever. Amen.

10. Catholic Sacramentals

Because of its belief in Jesus as the Son of God made man, the church believes that the whole of creation has been touched or graced by his presence, and is therefore holy. Certain things are used by Catholics in their private, devotional prayer life as reminders of this. These are different from the sacraments in that they are purely personal. They do not reflect the faith as do the sacraments. They are called sacramentals and include a wide variety of devotional objects, such as pictures, statues, crucifixes, holy water, and palms.

Gestures and signs also aid devotion by reminding us, at an unconscious level, of central elements of belief. For instance, touching holy water and making the sign of the cross on entering church links the ideas of the cleansing new life of baptism with the name of the Holy Trinity, symbolically disposing us to enter a holy space.

The custom of tracing the cross with the thumb over forehead, lips, and heart before hearing the gospel during Mass reminds us to attune our thoughts, words, and feelings to the Word we shall encounter in the reading.

Anything that helps people to pray becomes part of the rich treasury of the church's life on which following generations may draw.

The Place of Candles

Candles play a large part in Catholic culture. They burn with a living flame, and so indicate life. As a symbol of the new and risen life of Jesus, the special Easter or Paschal candle is used. At Mass, candles on the altar are lit to symbolize Jesus as the light of the world, and to link our present-day eucharists with those of the early church. Candles help to create a sense of occasion. They used to be carried in procession before the Roman Emperors as a mark of respect, as today they are carried before the book of the gospels.

Candles may also be used to symbolize a particular prayer, in which case they are called votive candles, and are usually lit in front of the statue of Mary or one of the saints whose help is being sought.

Saints of the Church

Though not a sacramental per se, belief in the saints and their intercessory power has always been part of the Catholic tradition. In the New Testament, "saints" simply meant followers of Christ. Today the term is applied to those who are already in heaven. They, and particularly Mary, the mother of Jesus, have played a large part in Catholic belief and culture. Their importance stems from the Catholic way of seeing the church as a family that stretches back in time, and includes those who have lived and died before us and who are now enjoying the direct presence of God. If we value someone in life and pray for their well-being, it seems natural to continue to do so after their death, and also to enlist their prayers for us.

Catholics also believe that there are those who have died for whom we still need to pray. These people are in Purgatory. Until we die, we won't know exactly what life is like after death. So we are obliged to use the language and imagery of what we do know well in order to help us make sense of this mystery. We know that to come into the direct presence of God (being in heaven), we need to be released from whatever selfishness and sin still clings to us and disfigures us at death, for (of heaven) "nothing unclean will enter it" (Rv 21:27).

This process of release, or "purging," is seen by Christians of the Eastern tradition as one of growth towards maturity, while in the West, the language is more like that of a legal sentence. We pray during Mass for those who have died: "Bring them and all the departed into the light of your presence" (*Eucharistic Prayer II*).

This popular and ancient prayer is addressed to the church's number one saint, Mary. The greetings to Mary by the Archangel Gabriel and by Elizabeth in Luke 1:28 and 42 form the first half of this prayer, which was in use by Christians of the fifth century: "Hail Mary, full of grace. The Lord is with you. Blessed are you among women and blessed is the fruit of your womb, Jesus."

The "Hail Mary"

The second half, added and in use by the sixteenth century, petitions Mary to pray on our behalf. The term "mother of God" reminds us of both the humanity and the divinity of Jesus. By saying "us sinners" we are acknowledging our own share in the world's suffering and our solidarity with each other: "Holy Mary, mother of God, pray for us sinners, now and at the hour of our death. Amen."

To pray the rosary is to be engaged in prayer at many levels. Spoken prayers are counted off by means of beads strung in a particular pattern. Meanwhile, the imagination is involved in meditating on each of the fifteen mysteries, or events in the life, death, and resurrection of Christ Jesus seen, as it were, through his mother's eyes. The fifteen subjects are grouped into three sections:

The Rosary

•the joyful mysteries, concerning the birth and early life of Jesus;

•the sorrowful, focusing on his suffering and death;

•the glorious, involved with the resurrection and its consequences.

Each of these sections is made up of five specific events. Each event is contemplated during the recitation of the *Lord's Prayer* and ten *Hail Marys*, one bead counted off with every prayer. The sequence of ten *Hail Marys*, called a decade, is concluded with a *Glory be...* (to the Father, and to the Son and to the Holy Spirit, as it was in the beginning, is now and ever shall be, world without end. Amen.).

By the time you have prayed your way around the

rosary once, you will have said five decades and pondered five mysteries. To pray the complete rosary you would go around it three times, saying altogether fifteen *Our Fathers,* fifteen *Glory Bes,* and one hundred and fifty *Hail Marys.* This devotion, or form of prayer, was developed by people in the Middle Ages who wished to join the monks in reciting the 150 psalms which they prayed regularly, but, as the ordinary people could not read Latin, they joined with the monks by repeating the *Hail Mary* instead.

The Group Session

Beforehand, arrange to visit your parish church as a group. If this is not possible, invite someone to talk about the sacramentals found there. In your large group, welcome everyone and then take a guided tour of the parish church, pointing out specific items and explaining their role. Try to include the sacristy and confessionals. A display of vestments and altar furniture may also be of interest. Even life-long Catholics may value such an exploration!

If time permits after the tour, review the theme of this session, picking up comments and questions from the group. Once in small groups, offer these topics for discussion:

•What helps you to remember your loved ones?

•In prayer, is it easier for you to address someone you can see represented by a picture or statue?

•How necessary or desirable do you think it is for "holy art" to be of a high standard?

•How comfortable do you feel with certain Catholic sacramentals? Do any of them bother or puzzle you?

•Do you feel that too much or too little attention is paid to sacramentals?

•Which other Catholic practices would you like to have explained?

Back in your large group, deal with questions or comments arising from the small group discussions.

Begin by praying the *Our Father* (traditional version) together. Then, in silence, each person should say it to him/herself *slowly*. Then, all say it together word by word, or phrase by phrase, *very* slowly, pausing between each phrase. Eventually, when each word has had time to soak in, just be still, and allow time for members to ponder any words or phrases that come into their minds.

After a suitable period (as long as can be sustained), conclude by invoking the help of Our Lady, by everyone saying together the *Hail Mary*.

> Hail Mary, full of grace,
> the Lord is with you.
> Blessed are you among women,
> and blessed is the fruit of your womb, Jesus.
> Holy Mary, mother of God, pray for us sinners,
> now and at the hour of our death. Amen.

Closing Prayer

11. The Place of Prayer

In the Bible we find the story of God seeking to bring about human fulfillment throughout history. Sometimes God is pictured as a jealous lover looking over an unfaithful spouse; sometimes as a keen gardener, a vinekeeper who lavishes time on a favorite plant, only to find that it produces little fruit; at other times God is seen as a shepherd who cares for his sheep with love. Throughout the Scriptures God is seen as caring for all created things with deep love, and God invites humanity to respond with love and care.

In our lives the unfolding story of this relationship with God is called prayer. It is our response to the God who is already looking for us and waiting eagerly to embrace us. In prayer we do not force God to listen to us; instead we try to make ourselves available to God, to listen, to allow God to speak to us. Prayer is always God's work more than it is our own. God draws us, and not the other way around.

God is always closer to us than we can imagine. In prayer we try to open up ourselves to God. Anything that expresses our relationship with God, any thought or action, is prayer. God is not out to deceive or trick us; God loves us, and so we surrender ourselves in love. This surrender is also prayer.

The Prayer of Jesus

The way Jesus prayed brings a new dimension to our prayer. In the gospels he addresses God with ease, with intimacy, and with a name. The Jews refused, out of respect, to use God's name, but Jesus calls God "Father" with a word that appears in our language as "Daddy" (Abba). Jesus chats to the Father like a child, always with confidence, secure in the knowledge of the Father's love. At times he asks the Father to change his plans, as in his prayer in the garden at Gethsemane, but always he puts what the Father wants before his own fears.

Jesus' own way of praying was taken up by the church and kept for us in what we today call the *Lord's Prayer* (the Our Father). It is full of confidence that God is a loving Father, who listens to his children. The church teaches that Jesus' whole life was a prayer to the Father. The supreme moment of prayer was that of Jesus on the cross when his prayer then was the voice of prayer of all humanity. As the one mediator between God and people, Christ's prayer is always heard. When we join our prayers to his, we can be sure that our prayer finds acceptance. For this reason all the official prayers of the church finish with the words "through Christ." Paul describes the Spirit as bringing about our closeness to Jesus. He says that the Spirit leads us to imitate the prayer of Jesus, and so we too can come to trust God as a loving Father, anxious to give us all we need.

Ways to Pray

When we pray consciously, that is by giving time to it apart from our living and acting, we can pray with praise and thanksgiving. That means to speak to God as the creator, to see ourselves as part of God's plan. We can pray with contrition; that is, to admit our failure to live as part of this plan. We can pray with petition, meaning that we become more sensitive to the needs of others, and more sensitive to the ways in which we can help them.

Catholic Christians pray as a people whom God has called, and so we pray as part of a large family. This is expressed best of all at Mass: the eucharist (which means thanksgiving), is the great expression of thanks from the church to the Father through Christ.

"This liturgy (or public worship) is the summit towards which the activity of the church is directed; it is also the fount from which all her power flows" (*Sacred Liturgy*, n. 10). By celebrating the eucharist and the Divine Office, "the church is ceaselessly engaged in praising the Lord and interceding for the salvation of the entire world" (*Sacred Liturgy*, n. 83).

The Divine Office is the official public prayer of the church, which is prayed at various times throughout the day. These times are Matins with Lauds (morning prayer), Prime, Terce, Sext, None (said between morning and evening), Vespers (evening prayer) and Compline (night prayer). Each prayer follows a fixed structure of psalms, Scripture readings, hymns, and intercessions. Over a four-week period, all the psalms in the Bible will have been said, sung, chanted, or read silently by priests, religious sisters and brothers, and laypeople, either in groups or by themselves. At any time, someone somewhere in the world will be offering God due praise!

In your large group, welcome everyone; review the theme. Invite team members (or others) to offer very brief explanations of different forms of prayer as experienced and practiced by Catholics today. Examples might include: charismatic prayer; meditation on Scripture (Lord's Prayer, titles of God, etc.); healing prayer (e.g., of memories); intercessory prayers (prayer of the faithful); the rosary; litanies; the stations of the cross; the Jesus Prayer

In your small groups, discuss the following questions:

•Is there a way of prayer that you have found to be helpful? What is it and why does it appeal to you?

•What difficulties do you find with prayer?

•Is it more important to you to "say prayers" or "to pray"?

•When may knowing a number of formula prayers be helpful? Which do you cherish and why?

•Have there been circumstances in your life that have been affected by prayer?

•Can you pray "among the pots and pans" (as St. Teresa of Avila expressed it), or do you need a special time and place?

The Group Session

Back again in the large group, take comments or questions from the small groups. Deal with any practical matters. Begin by inviting each person to pray quietly in his/her own way for five minutes or so.

Then conclude with praying together the Magnificat:

Closing Prayer

My soul glorifies the Lord, my spirit rejoices in God, my Savior. You have looked on your servant in her lowliness: henceforth all ages will call me blessed. You, the almighty, work marvels for me. Holy is your name! Your mercy is from age to age, on those who fear you. You put forth your arm in strength, and scatter the proud-hearted. You cast the mighty from their thrones, and raise the lowly. You fill the starving with good things and send the rich away empty. You protect Israel, your servant, remembering your mercy, the mercy promised to our fathers, to Abraham and his children forever. Amen.

12. Sign and Sacrament

When Robert Burns wrote "My love is like a red, red rose," he was not implying that his beloved was bright crimson. Rather he was saying that how he feels when he sees a lovely rose in June, is how he feels when he sees his beloved. The most intimate and personal things are often best expressed in this way, that is, by symbolic words or by signs or gestures. We greet people by shaking their hands; we express affection with a kiss; we show anger with a clenched fist. All of these are part of our symbolic language.

Signs and Symbols

The church has a similar symbolic language when speaking about God; it is a language of signs and symbols, a sacramental language. We believe that God cannot be seen by humans, but that we have been given a sign of God in Jesus, whom St. Paul calls the "image of the unseen God," and so we say that Jesus is the sacrament of God, that is, the sign or token by which God is present to us.

Christian art also helps us by expressing in images the same truth that the gospels communicate in words. "We declare that we preserve intact all the written and unwritten traditions of the church which have been entrusted to us. One of these traditions consists in the production of representational artwork, which accords with the history of the preaching of the gospel. For it confirms that the incarnation of the Word of God was real and not imaginary" (*Council of Nicaea II*).

Listening to the words of Scripture and of prayer, singing hymns, contemplating sacred art, and being involved in symbolic gestures and actions, all help to take our minds and hearts beyond our immediate concerns, so that we can enter more deeply into the celebrations of the mystery of Christ.

We need to be careful not to use the words "sign," "symbol," and "token" as meaning something that is not quite true. "It's only a symbol, or a token gesture." These phrases often mean that something is slightly false, or less than real. When the church uses its sacramental language it means that it is trying to express something very real and powerful by means of a sign. Symbol is the deepest form of reality.

More Than Gestures

Just as we believe Jesus to be the sacrament of God (i.e., the best way of making God present to us), so Catholics say that the church is the sacrament of Christ. That means that we will find the clearest expression of his life and work in the church, which is his body, through which he acts and speaks and heals and reconciles and gives life.

The word sacrament for Catholics has now come to describe certain activities of the church that express the presence of Christ acting in her. There are seven of these activities in the Catholic church: baptism, confirmation, eucharist, penance (reconciliation), orders, marriage, and anointing of the sick.

Seven Great Signs

The sacraments, therefore, are the signs that express our faith in the reality hidden underneath them. They are the signs through which we worship and encounter God intimately. They are the signs of the unity of the church, because they express what the whole church believes, not just our private devotions. They are the signs of Christ being present in his body, the church. They provide opportunities for celebrating the presence of God in the significant times of our life and in the life of the church.

The seven sacraments were defined as such by St. Thomas Aquinas, and subsequently by the Council of Trent in the sixteenth century. The form of each sacrament has altered many times down the ages, the most recent renewal being undertaken after the Second Vatican Council in the 1960s.

Actions and Words

Each sacrament consists of an activity accompanied by prayer, e.g., baptism is the washing with water in the name of the Trinity; anointing is a rubbing with oil, accompanied by a prayer of healing. This is the essential part of a sacrament: the activity with the words. The ceremonial way in which this activity is presented will vary from age to age and culture to culture. The sacraments are always public celebrations belonging to the whole community of the church. They are not private devotions.

Even sacraments that do not *seem* to affect anybody else (for example, penance or healing) really do. As everyone who has been baptized (or entered into the process leading to baptism) has been made part of the one body, one family of Christ, then the whole body is affected by the state of health of every single member of it, just as a speck of dirt in the eye, or a toothache, can bring low the sturdiest of persons.

Years ago, Christian writer Tad Guzie described a sacrament as a festive action in which Christians assemble to celebrate their lived experience and to call to heart their common story. The action is a symbol of God's care for us in Christ. Enacting the symbol brings us closer to one another in the church and to the Lord who is there for us.

The Group Session

In your large group, welcome everyone and review the theme. In a brainstorming session, encourage members to share responses to the following questions:

•What are some of the symbols used in everyday life?

•What are they saying (in ways other than in words)?

•What celebrations publicly affirm a matter of significance in the life of a nation, community, family, or personal life? Are they ritualized in any way? What effects are they intended to have on the participants?

In your small groups, suggest that the following questions be discussed:

•Are you able to celebrate special occasions within your family? Does your family ever share a meal together?

•Have you ever experienced a real sense of celebration at a civic or religious service?

•Does the use of symbols help you to celebrate? If so, how?

•Sacraments provide us with occasions for celebrating God's presence. In what other ways can we celebrate God's presence in our lives?

Back once again in your large group, take questions and comments from the small groups. Invite suggestions for symbols that people would like to explore, e.g., water, oil, wedding rings, the sign of the cross, etc. (These may be dealt with more fully in future sessions, but now would be an appropriate time to emphasize their symbolic meanings.)

Closing Prayer

Use a common symbol (a lighted candle, an open Bible, a cross) as the focus for reflection. Set it where all can see it. Remove other distractions, and invite everyone to concentrate on this symbol, thanking God while allowing the symbol to work silently upon them. Some quiet background music may be helpful.

Or, give all present the opportunity to choose a symbol (picture, cross, etc.) from a selection that you have put out before them, and then to concentrate on their prayer, using the symbol to focus their attention.

Encourage them to talk quite naturally to God as they pray. After a while, invite any who wish to do so, to share an insight or reflection. Conclude with everyone saying together this *Prayer of St. Ignatius*:

Teach us, Good Lord,
to serve you as you deserve;
to give and not to count the cost,
to fight and not to heed the wounds,
to toil and not to seek for rest,
to labor and not to ask for any reward,
save that of knowing that we do your will;
through Jesus Christ our Lord. Amen.

13. Baptism and Confirmation

The word baptism comes from a Greek word that means "to bathe, dip, or plunge in water." The English evangelist Trevor Dearing, in a lighthearted moment, once likened baptism to the action of becoming a "holy tea bag" plunged into the water to enable "all the flavor to come flooding through!"

Seriously, baptism is laden with a wealth of symbolic meaning and significance. Water, which sustains life, can also kill. Being submerged in it, even for a religious purpose, can convey the impression of undergoing a form of death. Dying and rising as well as being ritually cleansed and purified; these images have all been used by the church to mark the stage of admission or initiation through total repentance and conversion.

In the gospels Jesus was baptized by John the Baptist. Many years later the gospel writers linked this event with what happened to the apostles at Pentecost, when the Holy Spirit was "poured out" on them. The early church thus introduced baptism in the name of Jesus as the way of receiving his Spirit, and thereby joining the community which met in his name for teaching and the breaking of bread. So initiation into the church was made up of the following: baptism by water, the outpouring of the Spirit, and sharing the Lord's Supper, the eucharist. This is still the pattern today. These three sacraments—baptism, confirmation, and eucharist—make up the sacraments of initiation into the church.

Initiating Believers

According to the Acts of the Apostles, large numbers of people were baptized with no preparation beyond a "profession of faith," the declaration of their belief in Jesus as the Christ. As the church began to face hostility and persecution, there emerged a structure for preparing people for initiation into it. In order to test the seriousness of a person's interest in the church, and also to weed out the possible entry of spies into the community, as well as eliminating as far as possible the scandal of apostasy (the public denial of Christ by a Christian), the church began a catechumenate.

This provided a lengthy period of preparation for prospective members. It celebrated their gradual acceptance into the community by means of certain rituals, until the solemn moment during the Easter celebration when they received the sacraments of baptism, confirmation, and eucharist together, and so became fully initiated members. There was also a long period of after-care for the continuing involvement of the newcomer into the life of the community.

After the year A.D. 313, persecution of Christians ceased and Christianity gradually became the official religion of the empire. Within a hundred years, the catechumenate was becoming redundant, as newly born babies began to make up the majority of new entrants to the church. This became the norm, especially with the growing feeling that baptism was necessary for freeing the infant from the effects of the sin of Adam and Eve: "original sin." So the practice emerged of baptism for newborn babies, followed some years later by confirmation, and, finally, eucharist.

Gradual Change

This was the situation until early this century when the pope wished to make holy communion available to children, and so the order in which the sacraments were received was reversed. Now the most common order for Catholics is baptism, eucharist, confirmation. The Orthodox churches give all three initiation sacraments to babies.

During the first four centuries, therefore, the understanding of the sacrament of baptism underwent a deep change: from being a public entry into a community of faith to being a personal need for the cancellation of original sin.

Reversing the Process

Since the Second Vatican Council there has been an attempt to reverse this process. Once more the necessity of faith is being emphasized. Baptism is the celebration of a living faith; so even in the case of babies there must be some faith to celebrate. Hence the emphasis on the faith of the parents and sponsors.

As well as original sin, there is also "original grace," which is a more ancient idea. This means that human nature, and everything about our life and this world, has been "graced" by the presence of Christ in it. He was a fully mature man, the perfect human being. He invites us to become more fully human, to accept the human condition, to journey through life with its risks and possible failures by living a way of life that he has shown us: a life that does not end with death. He invites us, in fact, to live our lives by the same power with which he lived his, the Holy Spirit. We receive this power to begin the lifelong journey with him through our baptism.

Also, since the council, there has been the reintroduction of the catechumenate as the normal means of receiving converts into the church. This means that their progress is once again the responsibility of the whole community and not just of one priest. Their gradual initiation is accompanied by liturgical celebrations until their full initiation takes place at the Easter Vigil.

The Bishop Confirms

Originally the celebration of the sacraments of initiation was led by the bishop in the cathedral at Easter. With the enormous increase in the number of Christians during the fourth century, the bishops delegated the baptism and eucharist parts of the rite to the priests. Each bishop undertook to supply the part where he lays hands upon the baptized, prays for the descent of the Holy Spirit upon them (again) with the special oil or "chrism." He was to do this as soon after baptism as possible, but in the conditions of the times, it frequently took place only after a period of years: this part became known as confirmation.

Bishops can now delegate priests to confirm adults during the Easter Vigil.

The words used at confirmation include: "Be sealed with the gift of the Holy Spirit," and so it was seen as a means of perfecting or ratifying the baptism of those who were baptized years before as babies. By receiving the indwelling of the Holy Spirit, the missionary dimension of baptism and of the church is given new focus.

Confirmation now is a moment when the church shows itself to the rest of the world as a particular kind of community (a community filled with the Spirit of God), which is dedicated to the transformation of the whole of creation by the release of the Spirit.

The Group Session

In your large group, welcome everyone and review the theme. Then invite participants to choose one of the two following activities.

1. Explore some of the images that could illustrate the stages of the catechumenate. For example:

An Exodus journey—a time of oppression and escape; passing through the Red Sea; desert wandering; time of testing, making covenants; crossing the Jordan; reaching the promised land.

Becoming an athlete—general training and fitness; trials, intensive training, and preparation for the contest; winning a title.

Marriage—dating and courtship; engagement, deepening the relationship in preparation for the wedding; enduring love; commitment renewed in daily interaction.

2. Explore the symbols of Easter and baptism, death and new life, with special emphasis on water, e.g., stories of Noah and Jonah and early church practice. (The early church required those being baptized to be submerged three times, after each confession of belief in the Father, Son, and Holy Spirit. It must have felt to the wet and sputtering new Christian that he/she was close to being

drowned! How might that experience teach them about dying to the "old self" to be born anew in Christ?)

In your small groups, suggest that discussion center around these questions:

•What gives you a sense of belonging?

•Is what you belong to open to others or closed? Does it matter?

•What might encourage a real sense of belonging in the church? Does it happen?

•How was your interest in faith/church membership first kindled? When and how did you make a real choice?

Back in the large group, take questions and comments from the small groups.

Closing Prayer

Invite all present to quietly read Acts 2:1–4, 17–21. (It may help to also have it read aloud by a good reader.) Remind everyone that such passages were written for them. Ask the group to consider in what ways this reading applies to them.

After an appropriate period of silence, conclude by saying together the *Divine Praises:*

Blessed be God.
Blessed be God's holy name.
Blessed be Jesus Christ, true God and true man.
Blessed be the name of Jesus.
Blessed be his most sacred heart.
Blessed be his most precious blood.
Blessed be Jesus in the most holy sacrament of the altar.
Blessed be the Holy Spirit, the Paraclete.
Blessed be the great mother of God, Mary most holy.
Blessed be her holy and immaculate conception.
Blessed be her glorious assumption.
Blessed be the name of Mary, virgin and mother.
Blessed be Saint Joseph, her most chaste spouse.
Blessed be God in his angels and in his saints. Amen.

14. Eucharist (Mass)

This, the third of the three sacraments by which a member is initiated into the Catholic Church, is "the source and summit" of the Christian life. The body of Christ is assembled to express its praise and thanksgiving in the best way available. All the other sacraments in some way contribute to and exist for this purpose. The body of Christ (the people) receives the body of Christ (the eucharist), to become more Christlike, more like itself. The Word which was with God (Jn 1) comes into the world again, both as the Word (The Word of the Lord) and as food ("for my flesh is real food," Jn 6:55). By actively receiving the Word in word and food, the Christian accepts the challenge to be Christlike, to love as Christ loves.

When Jewish people celebrate the Passover, calling to mind the ancient liberation-event of their ancestors, it becomes a "happening" in the present. They bring the past so powerfully into the present that *they* are the slaves being called out from Egypt. Present experiences of oppression are seen through a fresh perspective, and so faith and hope are rekindled.

The First Mass

In the same way, each Mass is making real, here and now, the events that took place during the Passover in Jerusalem in or about A.D. 33. The Passover supper which Jesus shared with his friends, with all its foreshadowing of death and resurrection, was invested by Jesus with new significance.

The breaking of the bread is a symbol of the breaking of Christ's body on the cross. Sharing the separate pieces of what had been whole speaks of Christ's sharing of his life with his friends, to make whole again the one Body. As grapes are crushed to produce wine, and as wine is poured out to be consumed, so the cup of acceptance, recalling the covenant, is given new meaning as God's new

75

covenant, sealed with Christ's blood, which "is poured out for you" (Lk 22:20). Jesus, the messiah, identified himself with the lamb which each household sacrificed. The blood of the lamb had been sprinkled on the doorposts originally so that the angel of death would "pass over" and leave the household safe from death. In the Mass, liberation and life is offered again, not for one group of people alone, but for the whole world.

The Mass Today

Mass today can be celebrated by thousands in cathedrals or basilicas, by parishioners in parish churches, by a few friends in someone's home. It may be in the open air, in a parish church or parish center, or in schools, hospitals, prisons, or factories.

The variety of ways in which Mass is celebrated is truly "catholic," representing the tastes and traditions of all manner of people. The many different Eastern Catholic Rites worship in ways which, to western eyes and ears, seem very close to the Greek Orthodox. The musical tastes or customs of one community might drive another to distraction! Whereas early Sunday morning Massgoers often prefer a "quiet Mass," some South American Indian Massgoers seem intent on being heard from the most distant mountains! Whereas Europeans stand for the gospel as a mark of respect, Africans sit for the same reason!

Whatever the differences in styles, what unites Catholics throughout the world is the real presence of Christ within their communities. For communion means not only being united with God but also with each other. The triumph of love, so dearly won by Jesus the Christ, is celebrated in the great thanksgiving which is the eucharist.

Mass is not "out there," but "in here." We are not called simply to look and listen, but to respond, to accept challenges, to risk being changed. We are invited to share with Christ in a "pass-over" from death to life, not for our sake only, but for the whole world. The faith of those who celebrate is both expressed and made real. The quality of our celebration will largely depend on the kind of Christian life we live.

The two main parts of the Mass are the liturgy of the Word (centered on encountering the Word of God in Scripture), and the liturgy of the Eucharist (encountering the Word of God in the sacrificial meal). Introductory and concluding rites serve as a frame for the two parts. In the Introductory Rites we gather together, then sing an entrance song while the priest and ministers process to the altar. We are greeted by the priest and then, to prepare ourselves for hearing the readings, we are called to repent (change course) and trust in God's mercy.

Liturgy of the Word

In the liturgy of the Word we then attend to the readings from Scripture: a passage from the Old Testament (usually); our response in the form of a psalm; a passage from the New Testament; and a gospel reading.

It has been said that hearing the Word of God is only half the experience during the liturgy of the Word. Listening to the Word is the other half and that requires both effort and a personal response.

After the readings, we learn through the homily how to apply the readings to our daily lives. Good homilies have been known to change lives! Then we stand to proclaim our faith, knowing that some have been persecuted for doing just that. We place our needs and the needs of the world into the hands of God through the intercessory prayers, believing that the prayers of the saints join with ours.

Liturgy of the Eucharist

The liturgy of the Eucharist begins with the preparation of the gifts. We bring bread and wine to the altar, forms under which Christ offers himself to the Father for the sake of us all. We bring gifts of money (the collection) which represent tokens of our work and our daily lives. God is then blessed in the words of an ancient Jewish blessing in thanks for the bread and wine.

Then begins the proclamation of the Eucharistic Prayer,

"a prayer of thanksgiving and sanctification, the high point of the entire celebration. The meaning of the prayer is that the whole congregation joins Christ in acknowledging the works of God and offering the sacrifice" (General Introduction to the *Roman Missal* #54).

In this prayer the church calls to mind all God's good works in the past and expresses her hopes in God's faithfulness until the end of time. The church represents the words Jesus himself used during the Last Supper and in offering himself for the salvation of all. The church calls on the Holy Spirit to enable us to share God's life as we share the sacrificial meal.

Past, Present, Future

The past, present, and future are all drawn into this great prayer as, at each Mass, the sacrifice of Christ on Calvary is renewed, though never repeated. The simple bread and wine have become the blessed sacrament, the body and blood of Christ. Then occurs the breaking of the bread. As the body of the crucified Jesus was broken for our sake, so, in the breaking of bread, we are given a sign to be broken for others. As we are all fed from the one loaf, so we are reminded of the need to be "as one" with each other. Just before the bread is broken, we say together the Lord's Prayer and make our peace with those around us (normally by shaking hands).

We then accept the Lord's invitation to eat and to drink, to receive the communion sacrifice in order to participate fully in the mystery. We respond to the words "The Body of Christ" and "The Blood of Christ" with our "Amen." This is both our joyful acceptance of Christ's life and healing spirit, and our acceptance of the challenge to become more Christlike, at whatever the cost. By its nature, sharing the Body of Christ in holy communion bonds us both with God and with the church, the body of Christ. It is the ultimate sign of unity.

In the concluding rites, after communion, we move naturally into areas of concern for the parish. At this time in some parishes, announcements are made about events, services, charities, and meetings. It is right that prayer should lead to caring about others, not only in the parish but beyond, wherever need is felt. Then with God's blessing and our thanks for having been together, we are sent out into the world like the apostles to "love and serve the Lord," which we can only do by loving and serving others.

Christ Is Present

At every Mass, Christ is present in different ways. He is present in the assembly of the people ("where two or three are gathered in my name, there I am in the midst of them"). He is present in the Word of God, the Scriptures, and in the person of the priest, representing Christ for us. And he is also present under the appearance of bread and wine.

The Symbol of Bread

We pray that the bread will "become for us the bread of life." The bread which we have made and offered will become the body of Christ broken for us on a cross, but because of that, leading us to share the resurrection. So we see that only by our being broken for others are we obeying his instruction to "go and do likewise." The life which the bread gives often takes us too by way of the cross.

One body (the church, made up of many people) is fed from one "loaf" (Christ himself). As manna nourished the Israelites in the desert, so this bread nourishes us today, yet making us also aware of the millions of God's people who have no bread, and who thus become our responsibility.

The Symbol of Wine

We pray that this wine will "become for us our spiritual drink," the drink which brings the Holy Spirit into our lives. Wine to Jesus and his friends suggested two contradictory images. It was associated with pleasure: "You [God] bring forth food from the earth, and wine to gladden the human heart" (Ps 104:14–15); with feasting in the Promised Land, and at the banquet to be prepared when the messiah comes, when "You prepare a table before me...and my cup (wineglass) overflows" (Ps 23:5). Jesus had changed water into wine at a wedding feast (Jn 2:1–10) to show that he was bringing in the age of the messiah himself; and feasting, eating, and drinking are often used to indicate the joys of heaven, where Christ's kingdom is truly set.

This kingdom, however, is also associated with suffering, violent death, and sacrifice. Jesus asks his disciples, "Can you drink of the cup from which I drink?" meaning, are they prepared to risk the sufferings which he will have to undergo? Just before his arrest and execution, Jesus prays: "May this cup pass from me." So when we receive the cup offered to us at communion, by accepting and drinking we are saying *yes* to this challenge. We will endure the consequences of being like Christ, even if it means being put to death.

Sick and homebound Catholics are being brought holy communion to their homes or hospital beds by priests, deacons, and by increasing numbers of laypeople. These laypeople have received training and been commissioned as lay (or "extraordinary") ministers of communion.

Communion services, led by laypeople, have also become part of the church's life. Frequently now when a priest is not available in a parish, a lay minister will conduct a service at which people can receive communion. This will contain many of the parts of the Mass except, of course, the eucharistic prayer. The lay minister has to use hosts (small wafers of bread) which have *already* been consecrated and stored in the tabernacle. (You can always tell that there are consecrated hosts in a tabernacle if there is a special sanctuary lamp lit nearby.)

Because there are fewer priests than there are Catholic communities, laypeople perform a vital task in leading these services, even on Sundays. In many parts of the world, this is the normal practice as a priest may be able to visit a community only on rare occasions. The church ensures that the faithful are not deprived of receiving Our Lord in communion.

Consecrated hosts are not only reserved in the tabernacle for use in communion services and for communion to the sick. Such hosts are not just bread, but are Christ under the appearance of bread. They are reserved so that people can pray quietly in the sacramental presence of Christ himself. Sometimes one of the larger hosts is displayed in a monstrance, a glass-fronted portable display vessel with a gold or silver frame, usually of a sunburst design. Many Catholics find that praying before a host is a powerful help to concentration and a constant reminder of God's self-giving love to us. Usually this display ends with Benediction, a short service originating in the Middle Ages, in honor of the Blessed Sacrament.

The Blessed Sacrament

Here are some of the questions that often surface about the Mass:

Frequently Asked Questions

1. *Is Mass a time for private prayer?* There is a sense in which people should be praying throughout the whole of Mass, concentrating on it. The time to pray individual prayers, however, is before or after Mass.

2. *Should there be silence at Mass?* There are breaks in the Mass for people to collect their thoughts and consider what has been said or done, and this is easier if the church is quiet. We should be tolerant of noisy children. However, we should also be sensitive to other worshipers.

3. *Can communion be received more than once on the same day?* As long as you participate in the whole service, you can receive communion more than once. You should not just dash in for communion, however!

4. *Why do some people receive communion in their hands and others on their tongues?* It was the custom for a time for communion always to be on the tongue, but now it is a matter of individual choice.

5. *Are people only receiving "half" of communion if they*

receive under only one species (kind) (i.e., only the consecrated bread or host)? No, communion is complete if only one species is received, but restoring the traditional practice of communion under both species allows for a more perfect re-creation of the Last Supper

The Group Session

In your large group, welcome everyone and review the theme. If possible, show a video or slides that illustrate what goes on at Mass. Invite participants to name the highlights of the Mass for them, and write these up (on a blackboard or a large sheet of paper) to reveal the shape of the liturgy for this group.

In your small groups, discuss some or all of the following:

•How might John 6 (feeding the five thousand) relate to the eucharist?

•How can we prepare for Sunday Mass during the week?

•How can we describe the difference between "going to Mass" and "experiencing the eucharist?"

•Which symbols (including words and gestures) do you find helpful? confusing?

•Do any of the following seem to be given more or less emphasis at the Masses you attend: sacrifice, meal, celebration, community?

Back in the large group, take comments or questions from the small groups.

Closing Prayer

With a prayerful attitude, read the following four actions of the liturgy of the Eucharist. Don't move on to the next until you have given participants sufficient time to reflect.

1. The priest takes bread and wine.

2. He gives God thanks for the bread and wine in the Eucharistic Prayer, and asks for God to bless the bread and wine so that they may become the body and blood of Christ.

3. The priest breaks the bread.

4. The priest shares it with the disciples of today.

Conclude with everyone saying together the *Anima Christi* (or *Soul of Christ:*)

Soul of Christ, sanctify me.
Body of Christ, fill me.
Blood of Christ, save me.
Water from the side of Christ, wash me.
Passion of Jesus, strengthen me.
O good Jesus, hear me.
Let me not be separated from you.
From the malicious enemy defend me.
In the hour of my death, call me,
and bid me come to you,
that with your saints I may praise you
for ever and ever. Amen.

15. Reconciliation and Anointing

(Note: Since the sacrament of reconciliation frequently generates a great deal of discussion, you may wish to plan taking each of the healing sacraments separately.)

Being a Christian involves the whole of our lives. God loved us into existence as whole beings, as precious, free, responsible living souls. We have been made responsible for all that we do in this world. God inspires and guides us, but the choices we make are ours. From the beginning, God's friendship (not interference), was offered. The created world was handed over to the care of free men and women. Had they chosen to follow the advice offered, paradise in the Garden of Eden could still have been theirs.

God Takes the Lead

Time and again God takes the lead in restoring relationships broken by us: the Ten Commandments, the prophets, the Beatitudes—all to guide, not to force. God respects our freedom, but does not leave us unaided: the Holy Spirit dwells within us. God's grace unites us with the Spirit. Christ's body, the church, nourishes us with life-giving sacraments, provides us with supporting communities, and helps us to be restored to wholeness when we have abused our freedom.

Jesus shows us how true freedom works. Despite extreme pressures, Jesus always exercises his free choice, in his case by choosing to do the will of his Father. In making this choice, he makes a choice for life, for full, absolute, eternal, wholeness of life. What of our choices? Do they lead us to life, or to "other gods" like money, prestige, success, luxury?

Do we pour out our time and energy on others—the hungry, the sick, the imprisoned—working for social justice and world peace? Do the choices we make while shopping encourage animal cruelty, pollution of the environment, the exploitation of laborers? Do we choose to drink and drive? To evade taxes? To waste company time? Do we work at building relationships within the family, the neighborhood? Do we talk to our spouse, or just criticize? Do we grumble and depress those around us? The list is endless.

Sometimes basic attitudes about ourselves can cause us to fall into traps that can poison our lives. Three such traps include:

Falling into Traps

1. Believing that we *should* be perfect and exceptional. When someone points out some little failing of ours, we immediately conclude that we must be *worthless:* "Poor me!"

2. Believing that we should be treated with considerable sympathy and consideration. If someone fails to go out of their way for us, we write them off.

3. Believing that we should live a good, comfortable life. It seems to us that everyone else lives a better, more comfortable life, so we conclude that God doesn't care about us.

The biggest trap of all is that of believing that we're too old, or too stubborn, or too set in our ways to change. And in a way, this is true. Left to ourselves, we can't! We have to live with the consequences of our actions, but with God's help we can learn to overcome those sinful, selfish drives which often have terrible effects. We can grow from the experience and, best of all, we can experience very personally the wonderful love and forgiveness with which God embraces us.

When Jesus encountered those whom others called "sinners," he reacted with shocking behavior! He did not scold, blame, or shun them. Instead he went home with them for meals, welcomed their friendship, offered them

Jesus Forgave Sinners

God's forgiveness. To him, they were "strayed sheep," hurt or ignorant brothers and sisters. Even in his agony on the cross, he prayed: "Father, forgive them! They do not know what they are doing." He saw beyond people's sinful actions to the sort of people they *could* become. He showed that where love operates, there is no room for resentment, revenge, or bitterness. New beginnings can be made, new life enjoyed.

Where love operates, people and God are brought back into friendship, reconciled. Where love operates, people will be reconciled with each other; systems of oppression, exploitation, greed, and conflict can be radically overcome, and the hunger for justice satisfied.

Jesus still encounters sinners, forgives them, and brings them new life. He does it now through his body on earth today, the church. At his first appearance to the assembled disciples after his resurrection, he sent them out to continue his work of reconciling people with God and each other: "Receive the Holy Spirit. If you forgive the sins of any, they are forgiven them" (Jn 20:22–23).

Once in a Lifetime

In the early years of the church, the sacrament of reconciliation was experienced only once in a lifetime, after baptism. People then tended to put off baptism for as long as possible! If you *did* commit a serious sin after baptism, murder for example, or betraying fellow Christians to the persecuting authorities, and you wanted to return to the church, you were an official penitent. Penitents had to undergo rigorous trials to prove that they were truly sorry for harming the community by their serious sins.

When the community was convinced that penitents were sincere, and would not betray or scandalize them, they would welcome them back into the church with a joyful service of reconciliation led by the bishop.

By the thirteenth century, Irish monks had introduced the system of frequent, private confessions, so that in 1215, the Fourth Lateran Council obliged every Christian to confess and receive penance once a year. Later, more frequent confessions became standard practice. Since Vatican II it has been possible for the whole parish to celebrate together both the pain of knowing how harmful our lack of love can be for our relationship with God and each other, and the joy of experiencing our reconciliation.

Through the power of the Holy Spirit, the church continues Christ's work of reconciling the world to himself, handing on to others the gift that she herself has received, the gift of having been forgiven and made one with God.

Through this highly personal sacrament of reconciliation, Christ continues to meet the men and women of our time. He restores wholeness where there is division, he communicates light where darkness reigns, and he gives a hope and a joy which this world could never give.

Choices Are Available

The church provides choices in the way confession can be experienced. Some people prefer to *see* the priest when they confess, others to have a mesh screen or grille between them. Some people make a habit of going regularly, even once a week, to reflect on their lives in the light of the gospel. Others prefer to wait until they have a serious matter to "get off their chests" or when they have a choice of confessors.

The church recommends that people keep in touch with the practice of examining their consciences, and that they celebrate the sacrament at least once a year. Serious sin certainly needs attending to within the sacrament of confession, whereas lesser sins committed or minor good deeds not done can be repented of and absolution received within *and by* the celebration of Mass and in prayer, particularly during the recitation of the Lord's Prayer.

Sin is not only that which we do ourselves, knowingly and willfully, but that injustice or corruption which we allow to be done because we do nothing to stop it. The "not doing good" is known as the sin of omission, by which all of us stand condemned in a society where geno-cide, torture, child abuse, cruelty to people and animals, environmental destruction, and many other evils continue unchecked.

As St. John writes in his first letter: "If we say we have no sin in us, we are deceiving ourselves and refusing to admit the truth; but if we acknowledge our sins, then God who is faithful and just will forgive our sins and purify us from everything that is wrong" (1 Jn 1:8–9).

Anointing of the Sick

Can we doubt God's concern and compassion for the sick, wounded, and handicapped? Jesus spent much of his time healing: restoring sight, health to paralyzed limbs and bodies ravaged by leprosy, repairing disturbed minds. He even caused life to return to dead bodies. His healing miracles were symbols of God's longing for our wholeness; words of tender love expressed in miraculous action.

Today God heals through the skills of doctors, nurses, and medicines, as well as by the loving touch of caring relatives, friends, and others. The faith community can also convey God's healing through the sacrament of the sick, a sacrament which "should be approached in a spirit of great confidence....We must believe in Christ's healing love and reaffirm that nothing will separate us from that love. Surely Jesus wishes to say, "I will heal you. And so be healed; be strong; be saved."

The sign used in this sacrament is one of anointing with specially blessed oil. This is the third time a Christian receives an anointing (after baptism and confirmation). For this reason this sacrament used to be called "extreme unction" or "last anointing." Unfortunately, it came to be equated with impending death. Indeed the sight of a priest approaching for this sacrament was a source of fear that could prove fatal for a frail patient!

Since the Second Vatican Council, the emphasis on healing has been restored, the healing of the whole body, mind, and spirit. Part of the prayer accompanying the anointing reads, "Through this holy anointing and his great love for you, may the Lord help you by the power of his Holy Spirit. Amen. May the Lord who frees you from sin save you and raise you up."

Emphasis on Healing

The sacrament is intended for the seriously ill and for the frail and elderly, and may be repeated as often as necessary. Whether or not a cure follows, the really important effect will have been the encounter or meeting with Christ brought about by this as with all the sacraments. A cause for celebration indeed! This can enable those who are facing death to do so with renewed courage and confidence. Death may appear a disaster, yet it is a door through which we all must go, knowing that beyond is the limitless love and splendor of God. Our present senses are inadequate to bear the full experience of perfect union with God. Death can be the ultimate healing event.

As with reconciliation, the parish family can gather to express their faith, helping the sick by their prayerful support in communal anointing services. The community of faith is also represented by the priest when he administers the sacrament on a home visit or at the hospital. Laypeople take holy communion to the sick and often spend time with them, bringing them the news of the parish and providing company and support. A community that does not care for its members when they are sick or elderly does not care for Christ Jesus, whatever fine words they might use.

In this session the small groups meet first. After the groups have gathered, welcome everyone and review the theme. Invite reflections on the following questions:

The Group Session

•Have you ever experienced the effects of conflict, division, or prejudice?

•When and how have you personally experienced reconciliation with another and/or with God?

•What are some of the "other gods" in your lives? Are you aware of the consequences of the choices you make?

•How do you answer those who ask "Why did God let this happen?"

In your large group, explain the process involved in the sacrament of the anointing of the sick. Invite questions and suggestions for how the parish community can better reach out to the sick and handicapped.

Closing Prayer

Invite participants to spend a few moments in silence with closed eyes. Say the following slowly and deliberately, allowing a pause between each sentence:

Picture someone with whom you need to be reconciled. See that person standing close to Jesus, with Jesus calling to you to put your hand in that person's hand. Imagine Jesus has one arm around you, and one arm around that other person. Praise and thank him for the life of the other person, and try to offer forgiveness.

After pausing for silent prayer, conclude with this prayer:

My God, I am sorry and ask forgiveness for my sins. By the help of your grace I will try not to sin again.
Almighty, ever-living God,
whose love surpasses all that we ask or deserve,
open up for us the treasures of your mercy.
Forgive us all that weighs on our conscience,
and grant us more even than we dare to ask.
We make this prayer through Christ our Lord.
Amen.

16. Priesthood and Marriage

There are as many ways of living as a Christian as there are Christians. The church is made up of all kinds of people: young and old, rich and poor, married and single. The important thing is that once a person has received the three sacraments of initiation, he or she is as much a full member of the church as a bishop or the pope. Everyone shares in the church's mission. This is not so much to take Christ to the world, as he is already there, but to reach out in love to the people of the world, opening their eyes and hearts to God and drawing them into one family of brothers and sisters.

The Church Offers Service

To accomplish its mission, the church must be a body of people who offer loving service, who are aware of God's spirit in their lives, and who experience a deep need and longing to explore this with others. It is the church's privilege to provide the most perfect expression of thanksgiving, the eucharist.

Everyone who is a member of the church shares in the church's mission. For this reason every member of the church can be called a "priest," meaning a person who leads a life of service for others. However, there are different ways of being a priest. We have in the church people who choose to marry; those who live their lives as single people, and those who are "ordained." They are all sharing in the mission of the church, but in different ways.

The Ordained Priesthood

Some people in the church become its public servants through what is called holy orders by being ordained. Those ordained include bishops, priests, and deacons.

A deacon can be a man in his final year of preparing to become a priest, or he can be a permanent deacon, in which case he can be a married man with full-time secular employment.

A deacon's service is threefold, involving liturgy, the Word, and charity. Liturgically he may preside at baptisms, weddings, and funerals, and lead the people in prayer; proclaiming the Word, he may read the gospel and preach; for charity, he serves the needs of the people, especially of the poor, from right within the heart of the people. A deacon is ordained to assist the bishop, who may then assign him to some particular ministry in the diocese.

A priest is under the authority of either a bishop or, if he is also in a religious order, a superior. With a few exceptions, all priests in the Western church are required to be and remain celibate (abstaining from sexual relationships). In a sense their lives become public property and they become accountable to the rest of the church. They are the public face of the institutional side of the church.

The tasks of priests include proclaiming the Word of God to present the message of God's love and to enable people to explore their lives in terms of the gospel; helping, with others, to build up the Christian community; reaching out in service to the world outside the church; leading the Christian community in worship, presiding at the eucharist, and pronouncing God's pardon for sin.

Through the ages there have been different ways of looking at this priesthood. Sometimes a priest was a kind of judge, one who upheld the rules in the church. At other times he was simply one who did holy things and looked after the worship side of life, the one who acted as the go-between with God and humankind. Other ages have seen him as the guru, the wise and holy man.

All in all it is impossible to define exactly what the ordained priest is and does, because his life touches closely on the "mystery" which is at the heart of the church, i.e., the mysterious presence of God.

A Shared Ministry

Nowadays, priests share much of their work with laypeople in collaborative ministry (priests, deacons, and laypeople all working together), which is becoming an increasing feature in parish and diocesan life. The church recognizes that the gifts of all people, young and old, male and female, are needed both to build up the church and to serve the world. The range of activity expected of priests is markedly different from what was customary in times past. Often one of a team with members of his parish, the priest can nevertheless look to the New Testament for models of his role in the church.

First, he is a disciple, that is, he has heard the call from Jesus to "follow me." So his job is called a vocation. Being a disciple is the priest's whole life; he cannot be a part-timer. Secondly, he is an apostle. That means he is *sent* to serve others. His concern is to be for all people, not only for the Catholics in his parish. As an apostle, he is sent with authority to preach the gospel.

Thirdly, he is a presbyter. This means he has a pastoral care for a group of people. It is his role to organize and stabilize a community. His authority over them should not be one of domination, but of service. He represents the wider church to them, as he is the local bishop's representative and delegate. While he may work closely with lay parishioners, it is he who is accountable to the bishop for the care of the parish.

Finally, he is a presider: he gathers with people around a table or altar at which he consecrates elements of food and drink for the sacred meal through which God and people become one. In the person of Christ he absolves repentant people of their sins and anoints the sick and dying.

In all these ways, the priest acts in the name of Christ. It is Christ's mission in which he shares, that of building up the body of Christ.

Why Can't Priests Marry?

This is a matter which the church can change if the authorities wish, but of which there seems little sign of changing at present, despite much debate. Reasons for celibacy include the following:

Two Key Questions

Celibacy is one of the ways in which the priest takes on the undivided heart of Jesus himself. It is a challenge to love at the deepest level, a love without limits and open to all, a love that makes present the gentle power of the love of God. Celibacy is an opportunity to be really free in one's service of others.

When lived in love for Jesus Christ, it gives a person the inner freedom to cherish God's people with the love of the Good Shepherd. It leaves priests totally open and available for those they serve and frees them to move to wherever they can best be of service.

What About Women Priests?

Women share with men in the "common priesthood" of all the baptized, but they cannot be ordained into the sacramental priesthood. The authorities of the Catholic church feel that they cannot authorize a change from the unbroken tradition throughout the history of the church.

The precedence of Christ appointing only men as apostles is often invoked, although the Pontifical Biblical Commission did not find New Testament evidence to be decisive either for or against women's ordination. Symbolic language provides an argument against women priests in that the priest presides over the liturgy as the symbol of Christ himself (*in persona Christi*), the bridegroom of the church (see Eph 5:29–32). Thus the need for "natural resemblance" between Christ and the person who is his sign suggests that only men can be ordained.

The "Mystery" of Marriage

God is intimately present in the world, and there are certain things that we do that bring us into closer contact with this presence. Birth, death, marriage, sickness, eating and drinking: in all these activities it is possible to sense God's plan being worked out. Marriage is an important part of this mystery. In many ways it makes plain what the church is all about. It acts again like a visual aid. The official church could talk for all eternity about love and service, but unless we can see these things lived out somewhere in flesh and blood, we are tempted to believe they are fairy tales.

When two people commit themselves, in the presence of the church's minister and the parish community, to live together in love until death, they are promising to do something that is of great benefit to everyone else in the church. First, they promise to belong to each other and to work at belonging to one another, so that in a sense they cease to be two different people and become one. Their individual personalities can develop with the support of a loving relationship.

Second, they learn to forgive each other. They show that reconciliation, which is part of the mystery of the church's mission, is possible. In this they are similar to the priest, whose job it is to reconcile all manner of different parts of the human family to God.

Third, they bring healing to each other. All the hurts and damage which early life may bring can be repaired in the unconditional love that the couple has for each other. In many ways this is a second chance at meeting the unconditional love which parents have for their children.

Fourth, they share joy. They delight in each other, and so prove that the happiness of one can be increased by forgetting self and living to make another happy.

Marriage is also living proof of the cross. In real relationships, unlike those in storybooks, there is selfishness as well as self-giving, the wish to dominate or wield power as well as generous love, and the wounding word or silence as well as healing.

The specific issues of sexual morality which belong to marriage are dealt with in chapter 17. Here it is sufficient to see marriage as one of the ways in which the healing, reconciling work of Christ is carried out in the world today.

Can Catholics Remarry?

If a Catholic obtains a divorce, after marital breakdown, he or she is in no way barred from the Catholic community or from sharing fully in the sacraments. Before marrying again, however, the church, through its marriage tribunal, needs to consider whether the previous marriage had been a valid one or not. If not, then an annulment can be granted and the person may then marry (as if for the first time) and take a full part in every aspect of church life.

If the previous marriage was deemed to be valid, or if no annulment has been sought, any second or further marriage will not be considered valid. People in such an invalid union are full members of the church in every aspect but one: they cannot receive communion at Mass, though they can present themselves for a blessing. The church wishes to do two things at once: to uphold and encourage the sanctity of marriage and its lifelong commitment, and to offer care and support to those who have suffered the pain of marital breakdown.

The Group Session

In your large group, welcome everyone and review the theme. The leader should explain briefly the relationship between bishop and priest, priest and deacon; what each specifically does, as well as how their roles differ, overlap, and complement one another. If a priest is presenting this part of the session, he could share those aspects of the priestly ministry which he finds most gratifying. If members of religious orders (or third orders) are present, invite them to briefly share their particular "apostolate." Discuss how marriage preparation is undertaken in the parish. Could it be improved and in what ways?

In small groups, offer these questions for discussion:

•In his book *To Be a Pilgrim*, Cardinal Hume says: "Most marriages last and are happy, but all marriages could be better." Do you agree?

•Cardinal Hume also says that "Holiness consists in doing ordinary things extraordinarily well." What might he mean? Which ordinary things, and how?

•In what ways can we share in Christian priesthood in our everyday lives? Is it possible in your situation to proclaim the faith, serve the world, and worship God?

•What is the role of single people in your parish? How do you care for their particular needs?

In your large group, deal with any questions and comments from the small groups.

After a few minutes of silent reflection, ask one of your best readers to read Philippians 1:3–11. Then conclude with this prayer:

Loving creator God,
may we continue to be faithful disciples,
and may the good work you have begin in us
be completed through Christ Jesus, your son.
May our love overflow more and more
with knowledge and insights
that we might determine what is best for us
according to your will.
Guide us and be with us always. Amen.

17. Love, Sex, and the Church

A Christian chooses to follow Christ. This is the basic decision that determines the whole direction of a Christian's life. Every action and daily decision is inspired by the life and message of the person of Jesus Christ. Choosing, in the details of every day, a way of behaving that is Christlike is far more than simply following rules, checking up on what is allowed or not, what is sinful or not. Personal relationships involve a morality that is consistent with Christlike behavior. Cardinal Suenens once wrote that "Morality is a call to advance in the direction of what is good—ultimately, that is, in the direction of God."

Called to Real Love

Really loving relationships between men and women require a high degree of generosity, constancy, and unselfishness. Fortunes are rarely made from promoting such qualities as these. There are courageous Christians who are criticized by the media and society for not worshiping at the shrine of self-indulgent sex. Authentic Christianity will always be a "sign of the contradiction" in societies which promote other gods like money, success, and power. The deep anxieties which many, particularly young people, have about sex makes them easy prey for those who exploit these fears.

Whole cultures can be so steeped in "machismo" (an overbearing attitude of masculine "superiority") as to coarsen and brutalize the human personality and prevent real relationships of love. Love, for a Christian, is not a game, a contest, or a chance to dominate. Everyone is called to love regardless of the sexual element, and authentic Christian love, as modeled by Jesus, is based on respect for the other and concern for his or her happiness. All Christian morality is founded on this principle.

In order to be able to make right decisions about our relationships, a Christian should be aware of what is said, both in Scripture and in the teaching office (the Magisterium) of the church. We have not been left in the dark to guess, or simply to "follow our feelings" (notoriously unreliable guides!). The church has a long history of helping us to make the sort of decisions that ultimately safeguard our own and other people's welfare and happiness. The way the church teaches is by offering firm guidelines or moral norms. A moral norm is not primarily a restriction or a prohibition. It is more like a signpost or a map or a fence that prevents a disastrous fall.

Making Right Decisions

These teachings tend to be of a general nature, and cannot account for every detail of individual circumstances. Ultimately then, each person has the responsibility to consider each situation, prayerfully and carefully, reflecting on the concrete experience in the light of Christian principles and their own obligations and commitments. Only then can our consciences be satisfied that we are doing the right thing in our circumstances. And it is according to our consciences that we will be judged on the day when God, through Jesus Christ, judges our secrets (see Rom 2:16).

Deep within their conscience individuals discover a law which they do not make for themselves but which they are bound to obey, whose voice, ever summoning them to love and do what is good and to avoid evil, rings in their heart: Do this, keep away from that (*Pastoral Constitution on the Church in the Modern World*, n. 16).

Since the sexual instinct is one of life's most powerful forces, the Christian is naturally concerned to control it responsibly and not be mastered by it. What can never be lost sight of is that sexual behavior should operate only within the context of a stable, loving relationship. To separate sex from love is to do violence to the whole complex

Sexual Behavior

unity of the human person. At two extremes, pornography is to authentic sexuality what sloppy romanticism is to love; they are both cheap counterfeits, selling people short because they are not the real thing. Marriage is the appropriate relationship for the "real thing."

The total lifetime commitment of two people to each other is the right context for the expression of their total love for each other, sexual, emotional, and intellectual. Within the stability and warmth of that relationship new life can most happily blossom and mature. The church teaches therefore that intimate sexual activity is reserved exclusively to married partners. This may seem hard on all others, although there are many times even within marriage when physical self-control, chastity, is needed. Whereas for the unmarried the sexual expression of love is inappropriate, they are nevertheless called to love and be loved, to respond to others with generosity and unselfishness.

Life-Giving Love

Love by its very nature is life-giving. The creator's love brought forth creation. Love cannot be closed in on itself or it would cease to be, and become merely the mutual using of the other for personal wants and desires. Married love, therefore, can be expressed most fully through the bringing to life of children. Parents have the great privilege of cooperating with God's creativity in the building up of families. They have the responsibility and the right to plan their families, as Pope John Paul II taught during his visit to Brazil in 1980. In doing so they are to avoid being influenced by "the spread of a contraceptive and anti-life mentality."

The church teaches responsible parenthood, but the only method of family planning that receives her approval is the "safe period" (also known as the rhythm method). This is because the cycle of fertility and infertility in the wife is part of God's deliberate creation, and to take advantage of it does not conflict with natural law as contraception does. In recent years, research has made it far easier to make an accurate assessment of when the fertile period will occur.

The church has clearly declared her beliefs on the morality of artificial birth control. But this is not the same as automatically labeling people who do not follow them as "sinners," or determining the degree of blame incurred by individuals. Indeed this principle (of not judging) applies right across the moral field. Each of us is intimately answerable to God, who speaks to us with the voice of a trained conscience. The job of a Catholic is to "form" his or her conscience to the very best of his or her ability, according to the church's teaching.

Life and Death Issues

All life is a gift of God. All living creatures, therefore, are special, sacred, and precious. God shared our human life in the person of Jesus. All human life then, must be respected and protected absolutely from the moment of conception.

The church condemns all direct and intentional killing or anything that indirectly but intentionally brings about a person's death. (The only exceptions are in certain cases of self-defense or of legitimate defense of another's life or others' lives.) The principle is always the primacy of love and the sacredness of life. Genetic experiments on unborn babies or the destruction or harm of any embryo, other than by purely natural and unintentional causes, is considered to be anti-life, and so, unacceptable.

This logically should extend to any action which harms the body—the "temple of the Holy Spirit" (1 Cor 6:19)— or the mind: self-inflicted ill-health caused by smoking, excessive eating or drinking; reckless driving and unnecessary risk-taking; drug-taking and sexual promiscuity; pollution of the mind through deliberate exposure to pornography or sensationalism; and all things which prevent the fulfillment of human potential.

Christians have a very great responsibility, one that critics look for with often-justified cynicism, that these values should not just be upheld and defended, but made to work. This can only be done with great sensitivity, love, and sacrifice. It is not enough, for example, to condemn abortion. If a woman is to give birth instead she will need to be supported and warmly befriended. For the potential suicide to benefit from counseling she or he needs similar support and befriending. The Christian cannot honestly pray for good health while not taking steps to live in a healthy way.

The Christian community must seriously engage in the hard but rewarding work involved in improving the quality of life for all people, and in prophetically denouncing any attitude or behavior that lowers or destroys human dignity. Christians should be people renowned for their sympathy, kindness, and understanding: those who are the first to forgive, those who are patently reliable, honest, and genuine. Then others will be drawn to recognize that Christians really *live out* their claim to believe in the sanctity of life.

The Group Session

In your large group, welcome everyone and review the theme. Invite representatives of parish organizations to describe their activities in relation to today's topics. If you don't have speakers, perhaps you could show a video. Diocesan libraries or audiovisual centers often have good material on issues of Christian sexuality.

Invite discussion on the issues raised in this chapter. Keep in mind that few moral questions are simple or straightforward in real life. What stories can be shared to bring out the issues involved?

In your small groups, invite discussion of any or all of the following questions:

•How did Jesus treat sin and sinners? What examples can you recall?

• "The church should just tell us what to do. Our job is just to obey." How would you respond to this statement?

•How might someone have to make a choice between

two actions, neither of which is good? Would they inevitably be committing sin?

•Can conscience be wrong? How can we help ourselves/our children to form a true conscience?

•Is it ever possible to judge the extent of another person's sin?

•How do you react to these words of St. Paul: "I do not understand my own actions. For I do not do what I want, but I do the very thing I hate" (Rom 7:15).

Back in the large group, discuss what action the parish, or groups within the parish, can take to support those who are faced with difficult moral decisions.

Closing Prayer

When all are in the appropriate attitude for prayer, guide the thoughts of those present back through their lives to times when they have felt hurt, or were wounded psychologically and emotionally. Ask them to hold onto that painful moment for a time, while John 8:34–36 is slowly read aloud.

After the reading say the following: "Ask our Lord to heal that hurt, to set you free. Know that that pain has now been handed over. Imagine that the space left is being filled with warm, life-giving love. Praise and thank God for this healing touch."

Conclude with everyone saying together:

God be in my head
and in my understanding.
God be in my eyes
and in my looking.
God be in my mouth
and in my speaking.
God be in my heart
and in my thinking.
God be at mine end
and at my departing.

—Sarum Primer, 1527

18. Justice and Peace

At the center of Jesus' teaching lies the kingdom of God. What sort of kingdom does he mean? Not the sort of kingdom, surely, which is remembered during the annual telling of the Passover story, the harsh, tyrannical kingdom of the pharaohs?

No, God's kingdom means freedom from that. It means "good news to the poor, liberty to the captives, to the blind, new sight, to set the downtrodden free, to proclaim the Jubilee" (see Lk 4, Is 61, and Lv 25). The Jubilee was the 50th year, when slaves were freed, debts wiped out, and land leases expired, which avoided land monopoly falling into the hands of a few. God was understood as owning all land, with us as tenants, stewards of God's world.

This describes the kingdom for which Jesus lived and died. Its aim is to promote the kind of life for which people were made, the life of a free people, loving God above all things, and keeping God's commandments. The wandering, ragged group of ex-slaves whom God chose to show to the world this radically different sort of kingship was simply the least of all peoples (see Dt 7:7). The "least of people," the poor, the strangers, widows, orphans (today we refer to these people as those on the margins of society), have always been God's special ones, heirs to God's kingdom. Yahweh "who keeps faith forever; who executes justice for the oppressed; who gives food to the hungry. The Lord sets the prisoners free" (Ps 146:6–7).

The Lessons of History

The Israelites, rejecting the kingship of God (1 Sm 8:7), clamored for a king, "like the other nations" (verse 5). But their third king, Solomon, behaved so like a pharaoh that he left a country split and in conflict for generations. Eventually, foreign domination and exile brought that to an end. By the time of Christ, Israel, under Roman rule, bred various groups all seeking in their own way to re-establish the kingdom of God.

Among these groups were the Pharisees who sought the kingdom through the legalistic, scrupulous practice of religion; the Essenes who sought it by leading lives in communities separated from the "ungodly"; the Zealots, by attempting desperate acts of armed struggle (which finally brought about the destruction of Jerusalem, widespread massacres, and forced exiles); and, the Sadducees, by appeasing the authorities and trying not to "rock the boat" (in which they were positioned rather comfortably!).

Into this scene came a poor, pacifist layman from Nazareth, who mixed with sinners and outcasts and chose uneducated peasants, fishermen, and women to be his friends and followers. The Son of God "emptied himself, taking the form of a slave" (Phil 2:7). The Christ came from a long line of the *anawim* (the poor of Yahweh, the socially powerless who depended on God alone). Jesus, who broke down the barriers between Jew and Gentile, male and female, slave and free (Gal 3:28), created a new relationship between people, making all people brothers and sisters of one another, with him, and so with God. How we treat the least of our brothers and sisters will ultimately be seen as the way we have treated Christ (Mt 25:31–46), so closely does he identify himself with the poor and the oppressed of the world.

Jesus Broke Down Barriers

Open to Transformation

Every time we celebrate the eucharist, sharing in the broken body and in the blood poured out for us, we are opening ourselves to be transformed. We are asking for the strength to be weak and vulnerable. We are committing ourselves to sacrifice our lives in the service of others. But through the gift of the Spirit, we are also sharing in Christ's power to give life to the world, to establish the kingdom. Like Christ, as co-heirs to the kingdom, our "kingly" service will be in "washing the feet" of our neighbor.

In this regard, Pope John Paul II has written: "The cultural change which we are calling for demands from everyone the courage to adopt a new lifestyle, consisting in making practical choices, at the personal, family, social, and international level, on the basis of a correct scale of values: the primacy of *being* over having, of the *person* over things."

Like the prophets and like Christ, we are called to stand back at times from the world, to reflect on it, to assess its values. Our own lives too need to be judged against the standards of the gospel. This can be painful! The Word of God cuts like any double-edged sword but more finely (see Heb 4:12). There is no promise here of the comfortable, self-satisfied, nice sort of feeling that passes for "peace," for "really it could be a complete denial of what Christ meant by peace which sent most of the apostles to brutal death and was a terrific confrontation with the society in which they lived" (Dom T. Cullinan, O.S.B., *The Roots of Social Injustice*).

We Cannot Hide

The society in which we all live involves us as participants. None of us is a mere spectator. We cannot hide from our responsibilities to the world's poor and oppressed by barricading ourselves behind private worlds, for there is only one world, God's, in which we are but tenants. Over the centuries we have created systems—economic, political, social, and so on—through which only a few enjoy the benefits of the world's resources. When the church speaks up for oppressed people anywhere, she is not "dabbling in politics" but exercising her prophetic voice. She is proclaiming with Mahatma Gandhi that "the earth has enough for everyone's need, but not enough for everyone's greed."

Helder Camara (a former bishop in Brazil and a leading figure in the fight for peace and justice) notes the connection between the "structural violence" of systems which keep people poor, deprived, and oppressed, and the (often bloody) violence of those victims in response. Often one form of tyranny is simply exchanged for another and is itself frequently met by violent state repression.

With as much money being spent on arms in the world as on health and education together, and with three-quarters of all arms sales going to the poorest countries, the Christian commitment to justice and peace must be absolute. As Pope John Paul II explained in his encyclical *Redemptor Hominis* (n. 16): "We all know well that the areas of misery and hunger on our globe could have been made fertile in a short time, if the gigantic investments for armaments at the service of war and destruction had been changed into investment for food at the service of life."

We ask, "What can we do?" The answer might include the slogan, "Live simply, that others may simply live." This might involve not buying certain goods which have been produced at the cost of human or animal suffering. For a businessperson, it might mean not making decisions which cause prices to rise above the buying power of the poor or put others out of work. It might involve "acting...against all forms of domination, slavery, discrimination, violence...and whatever attacks life" (John Paul II). "Whatever diminishes, enslaves, or negates people is an offense against human dignity; it is also a kind of blasphemy against God" (Cardinal Hume to the Church of England Synod).

What Is Our Response?

It also might involve taking a more responsible part in community life, in the church, in trade unions, in political parties, in organizations and charities, or in education programs. It might involve restructuring our businesses and companies, devising new economic structures, and breaking down barriers between management and workers. It might involve giving "witness on behalf of justice by offering nonviolent solutions in areas of social conflict" (*Justice in the World*, Synod of Bishops, 1971).

Finally, it might mean giving to charity, sharing our goods

and time, while bearing in mind these words: "You are not making a gift of your possessions to the poor person, you are simply handing over to him what is his. For what has been given in common, for the use of all, you have taken for yourself. The world is given to all, and not only to the rich" (St. Ambrose of Milan, fourth century, in *de nabuthne*).

In a more contemporary voice, Dorothy Day says this: "The greatest challenge of the day is how to bring about a revolution of the heart, a revolution which has to start with each one of us. When we begin to take the lowest place, to wash the feet of others, to love our brothers and sisters with that burning love, that passion, which led to the Cross, then we can truly say, 'now I have begun'" (*Peacenotes, No. 4*).

Our Brothers and Sisters

Another church father tells us to act *now*: "What keeps you from giving now? Aren't the poor there?...The command is clear; hungry people are dying now, the naked are freezing now, those in debt are beaten down now, and you want to wait until tomorrow?...If we took only what we needed and gave the rest to those in need, there would be no such thing as rich and poor. After all, didn't you come into life naked, and won't you return naked to the earth?...You do wrong to everyone you could help, but fail to help" (St. Basil).

The final word is given to Pope John Paul II in an excerpt from his speech at Yankee Stadium in 1979: "When we Christians make Jesus Christ the center of our feelings and our thoughts, we do not turn away from people and their need....The poor of the world are your brothers and sisters in Christ. You must never be content to leave them just the crumbs from the feast. You must take of your substance, and not just of your abundance, in order to help them."

The Group Session

In your large group, welcome everyone and review the theme. Read together Isaiah 58:7–10. Invite a representative from your parish or diocesan peace and justice committee to talk about the work and goal of the members. Or invite a person from the community who is involved in a social agency, politics, business, a labor union, government office, or the like to discuss their work.

In the small groups, invite members to share stories of personal involvement in areas of active concern for the poor, elderly, handicapped, etc. Then invite them to reflect on these questions:

•What do you understand by "Christian peace"?

•What, if anything, struck you in this chapter as new, provocative, helpful?

•Can you suggest any *one* thing you may try to do *this week* as a result of this gathering?

Back in the large group, take comments and questions from the small groups.

Closing Prayer

Throughout the world, at noon each day, thousands of people say this *Prayer for Peace* (Satish Kumar). Say it together now, pausing between each phrase to enable the words to "hit home":

Lead me from Death to Life
from Falsehood to Truth. (pause)
Lead me from Despair to Hope
from Fear to Trust. (pause)
Lead me from Hate to Love,
from War to Peace. (pause)
Let Peace fill our Hearts,
our World, our Universe. (pause)

Conclude with this prayer:

Make us worthy, Lord,
to serve others,
especially those in need
and suffering from poverty and hunger.
May we freely share our
daily bread as well as our love and compassion. Amen.

19. Ecumenical and Interfaith Movements

Many older Catholics can remember when they were forbidden to worship with their Protestant neighbors. Although the modern ecumenical movement can be traced back to 1910, it was only with the Second Vatican Council that restrictions were lifted and Catholics encouraged to work and pray with other Christians for eventual unity. The council fathers also welcomed opportunities for Catholics to develop better relations with the followers of non-Christian religions. Centuries of mutual ignorance, intolerance, and mistrust—and even persecution—had to be sincerely repented and memories had to be healed.

Strides Have Been Made

In the decades since the council, enormous strides have been made. Most Catholics now realize that ecumenism, or the bringing together of the one household of Christ, is a vital part of their Catholicism. "Let us not delude ourselves that work for perfect unity is somehow secondary, optional, peripheral, something that can be indefinitely postponed" (Pope John Paul II to the Ecumenical Commissions, 11-23-79).

The restoration of the unity of all Christians was one of the principal aims of the Second Vatican Council, and it reflects the will of Christ himself that all may be one (Jn 17). Indeed, disunity is a scandal and a hindrance to the spread of the gospel. The church cannot fulfill its function of reconciling all people with each other and with God when it is itself unreconciled and divided.

Unity, however, does not mean "sameness." The variety of the Eastern Catholic churches can testify to that. While they differ among themselves in their liturgies, rules, and spiritual traditions, this variety "so far from diminishing the unity (of the universal church) rather serves to emphasize it" (*Decree on Catholic Eastern Churches*, n. 2).

The Catholic church comprises twenty-three autonomous churches, only one of which observes the Western, or Latin, Rite. The others observe specific rites derived from one of the six major Eastern Traditions: Alexandrian, Maronite, Syriac, Armenian, Chaldean, and Byzantine.

The Orthodox churches of the East have a different history, both from those which remained in union with Rome and from the Protestant churches of the West. With no dispute on matters of sacraments, priesthood, or the eucharist, Catholics hope that "with the removal of the wall dividing the Eastern and Western church at last there may be but one dwelling, firmly established on the cornerstone, Christ Jesus, who will make both one" *(Decree on Ecumenism,* n. 18).

May There Be One Dwelling

"Among those separated denominations in which Catholic traditions and institutions in part continue to exist, the Anglican communion occupies a special place" *(Decree on Ecumenism,* n. 13). Successive popes and archbishops of Canterbury have expressed their common desire to bring their communions into *one* communion of life, worship, and mission: "To this we are bound to look forward and to spare no effort to bring it closer: to be baptized into Christ is to be baptized into hope" (Paul VI and Archbishop Coggan, Vatican 4-29-77). To achieve this, John Paul II and Archbishop Runcie urged that: "The talents and resources of all the churches must be shared if Christ is to be seen and heard effectively."

With all the Protestant churches, Catholics at every level are expected to work, pray, and share. While theologians patiently try to solve the doctrinal problems, ordinary Christians are to do everything together, except that which conscience forbids. "Teacup ecumenism is not to be despised...every occasion of friendly conversation with fellow Christians enables us to share perceptions of truth" (Emmanuel Sullivan, *Baptized into Hope*).

Some of the things that local churches can do together include, as well as forming "covenants" and pledging themselves to share resources and pool buildings, personnel, and activities; working together through organized councils and fellowships. They can run pulpit exchanges, study days, socials, parties, prayer groups, etc.; jointly fund chaplaincies, schools, and missions; promote Christian involvement in the media, local radio and TV, and the press; foster groups of all Christians to study either each other's traditions or matters of common interest, especially Scripture; undertake joint projects for social justice, such as housing, unemployment, or race relations; and plan together to care for the elderly, handicapped, homebound, and others in need.

Prayer must lie behind all activities. "Prayer is at the origin of this movement; it accompanies, enlivens, and sustains its effort" (John Paul II). We do not have to wait for the annual week of prayer for Christian unity. Pope John Paul II reminds us that *every* Mass is a privileged occasion for prayer for unity.

The Spirit of Dialogue

The benefits of Christians getting together with those of other religions and opening dialogue or communication with them cannot be overstressed: "May I suggest that we must not only listen to each other, but together listen to what the Spirit may be saying" (Cardinal Hume to the Church of England Synod). Through this we discover how much we have in common with the other "religions of the Book": Judaism and Islam.

The Second Vatican Council reminded Catholics that Christianity itself emerged from the root of Judaism, and that as St. Paul himself says of his own people, the Jews: "They are Israelites, and to them belong the adoption, the glory, the covenants, the giving of the law, the worship, and the promises; to them belong the patriarchs, and from them, according to the flesh, comes the Messiah" (Rom 9:4–5).

"Since Christians and Jews have such a common spiritual heritage, this sacred Council wishes to encourage further mutual understanding and appreciation...by way of biblical and theological enquiry and through friendly discussions" (*Declaration on the Church's Relation to Non-Christian Religions*, n. 4).

Despite the close ties of faith between Christians and Jews, there has been a long history of misunderstanding and prejudice. Christians today acknowledge with shame and remorse the long record of crimes perpetrated against the Jewish people: pogroms and persecutions, killings and "ethnic cleansing." The church requires Christians to be sensitive in the use of language in interpretations of Scripture, in preaching, and in social gatherings, not to give rise to or to condone any anti-Jewish sentiment or bias.

The church also has a high regard for Muslims. The Vatican II bishops urged Catholics to forget the past, and to make a sincere effort to achieve mutual understanding.

The belief in the same one God, the common links with Abraham "our forefather in faith," the honor which Muslims show to Jesus and his mother, as well as their practice of prayer, almsgiving, and fasting, help to bond Christian and Muslims in so many ways.

True and Holy

With regard to other major world religions, "The Catholic church rejects nothing of what is true and holy" in all the great religions which have inspired and guided people's lives. While duty-bound to proclaim Christ, with whom we find the fullness of our religious life the church yet urges Christians to enter with prudence and charity into discussions and collaboration with members of other religions. While witnessing our own faith and way of life, we are encouraged to acknowledge, preserve, and encourage the spirit and moral truths found among non-Christians, as well as their social life and culture.

The church is eager to enter into dialogue with different

groups of people "in order to achieve either a greater grasp of truth or more human relationships" (Post-Vatican II Document *On Dialogue with Unbelievers*, 8-28-68). Among them are "those who respect outstanding human values without realizing who the author of those values is, as well as those who oppose the church and persecute it in various ways. Since God the Father is the beginning and the end of all things, we are called to be brothers and sisters; we ought to work together without violence and without deceit to build up the world in a spirit of genuine peace" (*Church in the Modern World*, n. 92).

The Group Session

In your large group, welcome everyone and review the theme. Invite participants to share insights into the admirable qualities found in followers of non-Catholic religious traditions (perhaps the ones they hail from).

In the small groups, some or all of the following may be helpful for group discussion:

•To what extent have we inherited attitudes of resentment or mistrust towards followers of other religious traditions? What stirs up these feelings? What leads to change?

•What is there in our language or behavior that members of other faiths may find offensive or discriminatory? Have we ever been hurt in this way?

•How justified are some Catholics in fearing that ecumenism may cause the loss of Catholic identity? Of what may non-Catholics be fearful?

•What are we doing to learn more about other religious traditions or Christian denominations? How important is it for us to understand the religious experience of others?

Back in the large group, have a brainstorming session to come up with possible ways in which relations with other religious traditions can be fostered locally.

Closing Prayer

Slowly and meditatively, read (or have read) John 17:11–26 (Starting with "Holy Father..." up to verse 26). After a period for silent reflection, conclude with everyone saying together this prayer, which is held in common by most Christians of whatever denomination.

> May the grace of our Lord Jesus Christ, the love of God, and the fellowship of the Holy Spirit, be with us all, now and forevermore. Amen.

20. The Christian Response

We have been called; we are responding. We are asked to be open to God, and we accept. "Do with me, Lord, as you will!" We offer our daily lives at the Offertory of the Mass, represented by the products of our work and our wealth.

Do we know, however, what we're doing? Just what may we be letting ourselves in for? There is always a risk that we may be taken at our word! That was the risk Jesus took in choosing disciples who might one day betray him. There is the risk Jesus takes daily, in presenting himself so humbly and vulnerably as a small piece of bread. To receive the full rites of Christian initiation—baptism, confirmation, and holy eucharist—is to accept the challenge of the gospel, to take on the risk of forming ourselves into the image of Christ Jesus.

Hearing God's Call

When Abraham (Abram) was called, he had to leave the security of his homeland for the uncertainty of traveling with no reservations made! (Gn 12:1–5).

When Moses was called to liberate the Israelites, he ran the risk of incurring the tyrant Pharaoh's wrath (Ex 3:7–12).

When Mary was called, she ran the risk of social disgrace and personal suffering (Mt 1:19).

The apostles were called to follow Christ and to share the Good News with all people. This required commitment, dedication, total service, and, in many cases, their lives. Is less required of us? Since the New Testament was written, the acts of the apostles have been written in the lives of Christians: in their blood, their work, their prayers, their service, their love.

We don't have to do everything. Fortunately for each of us, we simply make up the Body of Christ. But only when each of us does what is asked of us wholeheartedly and with love, can that body function effectively.

What Is Asked of Us

Our calling can be summed up by the three theological virtues: faith, hope, and love (1 Cor 13:13).

Faith calls us to an intimate relationship with our God. We have the responsibility to nourish that relationship through prayer, reflection, and a sacramental life.

Hope calls us to share the Good News with a needy world. We have the responsibility of being the image of God in the world today.

Love calls us to love with God's love. "Since God has loved us so much, we too should love one another...as long as we love one another, God will live in us and God's love will be complete in us" (1 Jn 4:11–12).

"Love" is not a warm feeling we get when we think of someone. Jesus washed dirty feet as an example of love in action, action that was shortly to take on the deepest dimension in his own death on a cross.

Ways to Serve

To what loving service are we Christians called? Some service involves the wider community. This includes teaching, nursing, and social work; visiting the sick, homebound, and imprisoned; involvement in local social and environmental projects; being active in national, local, and union politics; being a good neighbor: hospitable, open, and welcoming; being an honest worker, a fair employer, and a good companion; making a happy home.

Some service is to the parish community. This can include being a catechist with children or adults; being a sponsor or youth leader, being a parish councilor or pastoral assistant; being a babysitter or care visitor; offering transportation when needed; making coffee after Mass; collecting hymn books; running the parish charities and holding fund-raisers; organizing social events and parish outings; facilitating communications.

Some service is to the worshiping community through liturgical services. These include being a minister of communion; being a lector; being an usher, welcomer, or server; being a musician (organist, singer, guitarist, cantor);

being a "minister of the environment": flower arranger, cleaner, poster-maker, chair-mover, sacristan, and so on.

There is also the real service performed by countless millions of elderly, homebound, or sick people, that of prayer and intercession. Members of contemplative communities are as actively serving the church and the world by their prayer as are the busiest of parish ministers.

Service (or ministry) "is a function of the *whole* church. All Christians are ministers in virtue of the Christ-life they have taken on in the rebirth of baptism....Whatever we as Christians are motivated or inspired to do because of our baptism, in doing it we are helping to fulfill Christ's mission, spreading the Good News" (R.B. Kelly, ed., in *Called To Serve*).

Proclaim the Good News

Spreading the Good News is, after all, the church's mission and purpose. "Go into all the world and proclaim the good news to the whole creation" (Mk 16:15).

Remember those gifts offered by the three wise men to the infant Jesus: gold, frankincense, and myrrh? (Mt 2:1–12). Their gifts were a recognition that the Jesus they adored was king (gold), priest (incense), and destined to die a prophet's death (myrrh, a burial spice). With the sacrament of confirmation, the Christian is anointed to be "another Christ," anointed therefore as priest, prophet, and king.

These are not merely words. As shepherd-kings we are set apart to care for others, to lead them into Truth; as priests we are commissioned to minister to others to take the Word of Christ to them; as prophets we are called to speak out on behalf of others, to be fearless in opposing evil and wrong, at whatever cost—and, as myrrh signifies, for it speaks of death and burial, the cost is high. It can cost us everything and that is what may be asked of us.

The Group Session

In your large group, welcome everyone and review the theme. Read together, reflectively prepared sections of 1 Cor 12:12–13:13. Discuss the range of ministries available in your parish.

In the small groups, discuss the following:

•In what ways can we offer service to the parish? to the community?

•In what ways can we "proclaim the Good News to all creation"?

•Why are there so few committed Christians in our society? How can we reach the others?

•Could we show more joy, love, and liveliness in our worship and in our relationships?

•If St. Paul were to pay a visit to our parish, what might he later write to us?

•How can we continue to grow in faith, hope, and love?

Back in the large group, take comments or questions from the small groups. Discuss the question "Where do we go from here?" Will some of the participants be baptized at the Easter Vigil? Will some be accepted as full members of the Catholic Church? What should they expect at the Easter Vigil liturgy? How often will they meet with you after the initiation rites are completed? This may also be a good time to recruit volunteers for a range of ministries, or discuss how the parish can better support the existing ones.

Closing Prayer

Have someone read aloud Matthew 4:16–20, slowly and dramatically. Then pray in silence for five minutes or so.

Finally, conclude with everyone saying the *Grail Prayer*:

Lord Jesus, I give you my hands to do your work. I give you my feet to go your way. I give you my eyes to see as you do. I give you my tongue to speak your words, I give you my mind that you may think in me. Above all, I give you my heart that you may love me in your Father and all humankind. I give you my whole self that you may grow in me, so that it is you, Lord Jesus, who live and work and pray in me. Amen.

The Challenge of the RCIA

When the bishops at the Second Vatican Council promoted the RCIA (Rite of Christian Initiation of Adults), they were inviting the church to take stock of itself and unleash a fresh new energy into its way of life.

The RCIA is radically new (see Introduction), yet draws extensively on the past, simply by opening up the treasure that the church has long possessed. The primary focus is on the would-be Catholic. Yet the whole parish community is invited into vital and critical self-examination:

•Is our parish attracting large numbers?

•Does it seem to be worth joining?

•What impression are we making on the world?

•How can we become a warm, welcoming, hospitable community in which our brothers and sisters can hear the Good News?

Where parishes have accepted the challenge of the RCIA they seem to find new life: "The parish is charged with a new hospitality, an openness that was always there but not always viewed as a ministry. Evangelization is just a word unless parishes restore the catechumenate...Parishes that are not joining new members to their community around the table of the Lord are hiding the light that searches out the darkness, the healing spirit that challenges while it soothes" (R. Kemp, "The Catechumenate and Parish Renewal," *New Catholic World*, 222:1329, p. 184).

Where To Start

It may be helpful to make contact with a neighboring parish in which the RCIA is working. It is essential to buy the book of the Rites, and to study it closely. Bear in mind that your parish is unique and so are the people and the situations in it. You will need to adapt the Rites and all contributory material (like this book!) to your own needs. It is also essential to avoid "going it alone." The RCIA is an exercise par excellence in cooperation and lay responsibility. There is so much material available on the structure of the RCIA that only a sketch is appropriate here.

There are four unequal periods, or stages in this process: 1. Pre-catechumenate, 2. Catechumenate, 3. Purification and Enlightenment, 4. Mystagogy or Postbaptismal.

Stages in This Process

Stage one (pre-catechumenate) may take years. It applies to all who express any degree of interest or inquiry. They are called inquirers and can simply observe and question. Should they feel drawn to want to find out in more depth how Catholics "tick," with the view to becoming one themselves, they are welcomed into the catechumenate at an appropriate liturgical Rite of Acceptance and welcome.

Stage two (catechumenate), may well take months or years. It all depends on the catechumen or candidate and the community into which he or she wishes to be initiated. Catechumens (persons not baptized) will journey at least a year in the catechumenate period. Candidates (persons who have already been baptized in a Christian denomination), may take less time. Supported by the prayers and companionship of the community (and especially the sponsor), the catechumen or candidate follows the sort of process of learning/sharing sessions which this book suggests. The next major step is for the catechumen or candidate to make a serious commitment at the beginning of Lent with the Rite of Election.

Stage three (period of purificaton, enlightenment) takes place over the weeks of Lent. Prayer, reflection, and liturgical support all help to prepare for the big moment. This comes at the Easter Vigil, when all the rites of initiation are experienced or completed.

Stage four (mystagogia), is the "follow-up" to the events at Easter. It is, most intensively, the period from Easter to Pentecost, when the Easter Vigil experience is reflected upon, and the life of the community has begun to be shared more fully. This period never really ends, as a lifetime is too short to do justice to the task of growing and developing as a Christian. The benefits to those who have traveled this path are immeasurable.

One catechumen described the process this way. "The first thing I learned was that I wasn't alone in my questions and searching. I met good people who besides sharing questions helped each other find new meaning and purpose to life and religion. The catechumenate was great, not because it gave me something I didn't have, but because it helped me find the God who was with me all along and helped me to respond more fully."

The Role of Sponsors

The following is adapted from the invaluable and inexpensive *Guide for Sponsors*, by Ron Lewinski:

Each candidate or catechumen is put in touch with a personal sponsor, maybe the key person who led to their becoming interested in the first place, a friend, neighbor, or coworker. In many cases it is the parish team who will recruit a suitable good-practicing Catholic for the catechumen.

If you are asked to be a sponsor, you will be the most direct and personal link the candidate or catechumen will have to the community. You will not be expected to catechize the candidate but rather to share your faith and experience as a Catholic. The candidate will catch from you the life and spirit of the church. Your role is to be a companion, walking alongside the candidate throughout the preparation period; a guide, pointing to the Lord as the destination of the journey; a model of faith to show what being a Catholic is all about; and a witness for the community of the candidate's spiritual progress.

Recommended Resources

The RCIA Transforming the Church. Thomas H. Morris. Paulist Press, 997 Macarthur Blvd, Mahwah, NJ 07430. This excellent resource book won first place in the 1990 Catholic Book Awards.

The Basic Sixteen Documents: Vatican Council II. Costello Publishing Company, P.O. Box 9, Northport, NY 11768. Contains a completely revised translation of the documents in inclusive language. An excellent resource for catechumens and their sponsors.

Catechism of the Catholic Church. United States Catholic Conference, 3211 Fourth Street NE, Washington, DC 20017-1194. A very useful compendium of Catholic doctrine.

The following resources are available from Twenty-Third Publications, P.O. Box 180, Mystic, CT 06355.

Faith Alive: A New Presentation of Catholic Belief and Practice. Rowanne Pasco and John Redford, eds. This is a panoramic view of the Catholic church, its teachings, history, and tradition.

Catholic Customs and Traditions: A Popular Guide. Greg Dues. A resource filled with quickly available information about the Catholic faith, its customs, and practices.

This Is Our Mass. Tom Coyle. Ideal for RCIA use to explain the rich symbolism and meaning of the eucharistic liturgy.

The Gift of the Mass: How It Shapes and Changes Our Lives. Bishop Vincent Nichols. These meditations offer new insights about the liturgy for candidates and catechumens and also for their catechists and sponsors.

The following books are available from Liturgy Training Publications, 1800 N. Hermitage Ave, Chicago, IL 60622-1101.

The Liturgy Documents: A Parish Resource. Elizabeth Hoffman, ed. The most important and useful documents of the liturgical reform are collected here under one cover for reference and study.

The Catechetical Documents: A Parish Resource. Martin Connell, ed. Gathered in one book are all the major catechetical teachings from the Second Vatican Council to the present. Each document is introduced by an expert or scholar in the field.

Rite of Christian Initiation of Adults. English Study Edition (also available in Spanish).

How to Form a Catechumenate Team. Karen Hinman Powell. Practical steps for selecting, forming, and maintaining a strong team to support the men and women who seek Christian initiation.

Guide for Sponsors. Ron Lewinski. This classic has guidelines, activities, and prayers that will help sponsors as they guide the candidates, challenge them, listen to them, and share the faith with them. A helpful glossary of terms is included.

A Catechumenate Needs Everybody: Study Guides for Parish Ministers. James A. Wilde, ed. Each chapter describes a different task related to Christian initiation. The pages are perforated to allow duplication by the purchaser for use in promoting the ministries and guiding those who wish to serve in those roles.

The Role of the Assembly in Christian Initiation. Catherine Vincie, RSHM. What does it mean, as paragraph 8 of the *Rite of Christian Initiation of Adults* says, that the initiation of adults is the responsibility of all the baptized? How has the understanding of the assembly's role developed as the implementation of the order of initiation has progressed?

Eucharist as Sacrament of Initiation. Nathan D. Mitchell. Anyone who is serious about understanding the meaning of the eucharist will find much to ponder in this book.

On the Rite of Election. Rita Ferrone. Examines what the rite of election is all about. Also looks at where it came from and what part it plays in the order of Christian initiation.

Preaching the Rite of Christian Initiation. Jan Michael Joncas. Looks at the liturgy of the Word as the primary place where the formation of catechumens, and indeed all the faithful, takes place. The role of preaching is emphasized.

One at the Table: The Reception of Baptized Christians. Ronald A. Oakham. This is a comprehensive, pastoral plan for adapting the principles of initiation for the baptized candidate.

Sunday Readings

Cycle A

First Sunday of Advent
Readings: Is 2:1–5; Rom 13:11–14;
Mt 24:37–44
Related Topics: Day of the Lord,
Eschatology, Parousia, Conversion

Second Sunday of Advent
Readings: Is 11:1–10; Rom 15:4–9;
Mt 3:1–12
Related Topics: Baptism, Initiation,
Repentance, Conversion, John and
Jesus

Third Sunday of Advent
Readings: Is 35:1–6, 10; Jas 5:7–10;
Mt 11:2–11
Related Topics: Repentance, Messiah,
Advent waiting, Kingdom of God

Fourth Sunday of Advent
Readings: Is 7:10–14; Rom 1:1–7;
Mt 1:18–24
Related Topics: Role of Mary, Virgin
Birth, Emmanuel, God Is With Us

Christmas
Readings: Is 52:7–10; Heb 1:1–6; Jn
1:1–18
Related Topics: Real Presence of Jesus
in the World, Incarnation

Holy Family
Readings: Sir 3:2–6, 12–14; Col
3:12–21; Mt 2:13–15, 19–23
Related Topics: Fourth Commandment,
World Peace, Sexism

Baptism of the Lord
Readings: Is 42:1–4, 6–7; Acts
10:34–38; Mt 3:13–17
Related Topics: Call of God, Divinity of
Christ, Christology, Development of
Doctrine, Baptism, Salvation, Holy
Spirit, Violence, Peace

First Sunday of Lent
Readings: Gn 2:7–9, 3:1–7;
Rom 5:12–19; Mt 4:1–11
Related Topics: Creation, Original Sin,
Justification, Jesus' Self-Knowledge,
Humanity of Jesus, Choice and
Responsibility

Second Sunday in Lent
Readings: Gn 12:1–4; 2 Tim 1:8–10;
Mt 17:1–9
Related Topics: Transfiguration, Old
Testament Theology of Election, Grace,
Trust, Hope

Third Sunday in Lent
Readings: Ex 17:3–7; Rom 5:1–2, 5–8;
Jn 4:5–42
Related Topics: Exodus, Providence,
Grace, Self-Awareness, Faith

Fourth Sunday in Lent
Readings: 1 Sm 16:1, 6–7, 10–13;
Eph 5:8–14; Jn 9:1–41
Related Topics: O.T. Theology—
Election, King, Healing, Personal and
Social Sin, Social Responsibility,
Charismatic Dimension

Fifth Sunday in Lent
Readings: Ez 37:12–14; Rom 8:8–11;
Jn 11:1–45
Related Topics: Death, Resurrection,
Heresy, Christology, Healing, Paschal
Mystery, Belief

Passion Sunday—Palm Sunday
Readings:
Procession with Palms: Mt 21:1–11;
Is 50:4–7; Phil 2:6–11; Mt 26:14—27:66
Related Topics: Christology,
Soteriology, Storytelling, Symbol,
Justice, Passion

Second Sunday of Easter
Readings: Acts 2:42–47; 1 Pt 1:3–9;
Jn 20:19–31
Related Topics: Faith, Beliefs, Creed,
Doubt, Peace, U.S. Bishops' Peace
Pastoral, Entry Into New Life

Third Sunday of Easter
Readings: Acts 2:14, 22–28; 1
Pt 1:17–21; Lk 24:13–35
Related Topics: Eucharist, Journeying,
Self-Examination, Critical Reflection,
Liturgical Renewal, Risen Jesus

Fourth Sunday of Easter
Readings: Acts 2:14, 36–41; 1
Pt 2:20–25; Jn 10:1–10
Related Topics: Pastoral Leadership,

Economic Justice, Good Shepherd, Shepherding, Discipleship

Fifth Sunday of Easter
Readings: Acts 6:1–7; 1 Pt 2:4–9; Jn 14:1–12
Related Topics: Jesus—the Way, Truth, Life, Christology, Discipleship, Royal Priesthood

Sixth Sunday of Easter
Readings: Acts 8:5–8, 14–17; 1 Pt 3:15–18; Jn 14:15–21
Related Topics: Commandment of Love, Prayer, Christian Life-styles, Hope, God's Presence Within Us

Ascension Thursday
Readings: Acts 1:1–11; Eph 1:17–23; Mt 28:16–20
Related Topics: Call of God, Mission of the Church, Discipleship, Christian Hope, Role of the Holy Spirit

Seventh Sunday of Easter
Readings: Acts 1:12–14; 1 Pt 4:13–16; Jn 17:1–11
Related Topics: Prayer, Liturgy, Ecclesiology, Eschatology, Reign of God, Waiting for God

Trinity Sunday
Readings: Ex 34:4b–6, 8–9; 2 Cor 13:11–13; Jn 3:16–18
Related Topics: Love of God and Others, Building Christian Community, Social Responsibility, Mystery of Love, Trinity

Feast of Corpus Christi
Readings: Dt 8:2–3, 14b–16a; 1 Cor 10:16–17; Jn 6:51–58
Related Topics: Eucharist, Body of Christ, Ecclesiology, Personal and Social Sin, Conversion, Community, Bread of Life

Second Sunday in Ordinary Time
Readings: Is 49:3, 5–6; 1 Cor 1:1–3; Jn 1:29–34
Related Topics: The Value of Witnessing, Christian Witness, Holy Spirit, Trinity, Discipleship, Servanthood and Humility

Third Sunday in Ordinary Time
Readings: Is 8:23–9:3; 1 Cor 1:10–13, 17; Mt 4:12–23
Related Topics: Life After a Tragedy, Death and Dying, Suffering,

Forgiveness, Cost of Discipleship, Light of Faith

Fourth Sunday in Ordinary Time
Readings: Zep 2:3, 3:12–13; 1 Cor 1:26–31; Mt 5:1–12
Related Topics: The Beatitudes—a blueprint for Christian living, Vision of God's Kingdom, Conversion, The Upside-down Life

Fifth Sunday in Ordinary Time
Readings: Is 58:7–10; 1 Cor 2:1–5; Mt 5:13–16
Related Topics: Our Christian Vocation, Call of God, Social Encyclicals, Social Responsibility, Symbols of Salt and Light, Power Issues

Sixth Sunday in Ordinary Time
Readings: Sir 15:15–20; 1 Cor 2:6–10; Mt 5:17–37
Related Topics: Moral Behavior of the Christian, Moral Decision Making, Law, Christian Morality, Sex and Violence

Seventh Sunday in Ordinary Time
Readings: Lv 19:1–2, 17–18; 1 Cor 3:16–23; Mt 5:38–48
Related Topics: Nonviolence, Social Justice, Social Sin

Eighth Sunday in Ordinary Time
Readings: Is 49:14–15; 1 Cor 4:1–5; Mt 6:24–34
Related Topics: Providence of God, Christian Stewardship, Christian/Gospel Poverty and Life-style, Feminine Images of God

Ninth Sunday in Ordinary Time
Readings: Dt 11:18, 26–28; Rom 3:21–25, 28; Mt 7:21–27
Related Topics: Christian Integrity, Christian Discipleship, Ecclesial Conversion, Christian Witness, Faith and Works

Tenth Sunday in Ordinary Time
Hos 6:3–6; Rom 4:18–25; Mt 9:9–13
Related Topics: God's Universal Love, The Call of the Sinner, Christian Love and Mercy, Christian Call, St. Matthew, Concern for the Poor and Neglected, Salvation

Eleventh Sunday in Ordinary Time
Readings: Ex 19:2–6; Rom 5:6–11; Mt 9:36—10:8

Related Topics: Christian Leadership, Sacrament of Orders, Infallibility, Ecclesiology, Role of Laity, Christian Vocation, Gratitude

Twelfth Sunday in Ordinary Time
Readings: Jer 20:10-13; Rom 5:12-15; Mt 10:26-33
Related Topics: Christian Suffering, Martyrdom, Christian Hope, Gifts of the Holy Spirit, Courage and Fortitude, Fear

Thirteenth Sunday in Ordinary Time
Readings: 2 Kgs 4:8-11, 14-16; Rom 6:3-4, 8-11; Mt 10:37-42
Related Topics: The Call of God, Discipleship, Sacrifice, Dying and Rising in the Paschal Mystery, Prophecy

Fourteenth Sunday in Ordinary Time
Readings: Zec 9:9-10; Rom 8:9, 11-13; Mt 11:25-30
Related Topics: Faith, Conversion, Discipleship, Humility

Fifteenth Sunday in Ordinary Time
Readings: Is 55:10-11; Rom 8:18-23; Mt 13:1-23
Related Topics: Hope, Openness, Parables, God's Word

Sixteenth Sunday in Ordinary Time
Readings: Wis 12:13, 16-19; Rom 8:26-27; Mt 13:24-43
Related Topics: Last Judgment, Kingdom of God, Humility, Evil

Seventeenth Sunday in Ordinary Time
Readings: 1 Kgs 3:5, 7-12; Rom 8:28-30; Mt 13:44-52
Related Topics: Divine Inspiration, Revelation, Cost of Discipleship, Kingdom, Solomon's Prayer

Eighteenth Sunday in Ordinary Time
Readings: Is 55:1-3; Rom 8:35, 37-39; Mt 14:13-21
Related Topics: Miracles, Grace, Social Responsibility, Hunger, Meal of Love

Nineteenth Sunday in Ordinary Time
Readings: 1 Kgs 19:9, 11-13; Rom 9:1-5; Mt 14:22-33
Related Topics: Faith, Miracles, Faithfulness, Discipleship, Seek the Lord

20th Sunday in Ordinary Time
Readings: Is 56:1, 6-7; Rom 11:13-15, 29-32; Mt 15:21-28

Related Topics: Ecumenism, Salvation Outside the Church, Universality, Non-Christian Religions, Baptism, God's Mercy

21st Sunday in Ordinary Time
Readings: Is 22:15, 19-23; Rom 11:33-36; Mt 16:13-20
Related Topics: Papacy, Hierarchy, Apostolic Succession, Christology, Ecclesiology

22nd Sunday in Ordinary Time
Readings: Jer 20:7-9; Rom 12:1-2; Mt 16:21-27
Related Topics: Sacrifice, Hope, Paschal Mystery, Prayer

23rd Sunday in Ordinary Time
Readings: Ex 33:7-9; Rom 13:8-10; Mt 18:15-20
Related Topics: Christian Love and Responsibility, Social Sin, Self-Discipline, God's Graciousness, Prayer, God's Mercy, Listening and Hearing

24th Sunday in Ordinary Time
Readings: Sir 27:30-28:7; Rom 14:7-9; Mt 18:21-35
Related Topics: Baptism—Incorporation into the Death/Resurrection of Jesus, Forgiveness—Basis of Relationship, Mercy—Virtue of Christian

25th Sunday in Ordinary Time
Readings: Is 55:6-9; Phil 1:20-24, 27; Mt 20:1-16
Related Topics: Justice and Charity, Mercy and Forgiveness, A God to Be Found, Eschatology

26th Sunday in Ordinary Time
Readings: Ez 18:25-28; Phil 2:1-11; Mt 21:28-32
Related Topics: Free Will, Conversion, Penance, Virtue of Humility

27th Sunday in Ordinary Time
Readings: Is 5:1-7; Phil 4:6-9; Mt 21:33-43
Related Topics: Prayer, Kingdom of God, Eschaton, Virtue of Hope, Centrality of the Death and Resurrection of Jesus, Providence of God

28th Sunday in Ordinary Time
Readings: Is 25:6-10; Phil 4:12-14, 19-20; Mt 22:1-14

Related Topics: Models of Church—
Pilgrim; Life of Christian Service,
Grace, The Invitation
29th Sunday in Ordinary Time
Readings: Is 45:1, 4–6; 1 Thes 1:1–5;
Mt 22:15–21
Related Topics: Theological Virtues,
Trinity, Church, God's "Instruments"
30th Sunday in Ordinary Time
Readings: Ex 22:20–26; 1 Thes 1:5–10;
Mt 22:34–40
Related Topics: Love of Neighbor,
Conversion, Covenant, Golden Rule,
Cry of the Poor
31st Sunday in Ordinary Time
Readings: Mal 1:14–2:2, 8–10;
1 Thes 2:7–9, 13; Mt 23:1–12
Related Topics: Trinity, Incarnation,
Commandments of the Church,
Catechesis, Teachers and Students
32nd Sunday in Ordinary Time
Readings: Wis 6:12–16; 1 Thes
4:13–18; Mt 25:1–13
Related Topics: Life after Death,
Communion of Saints, Prayer, Wisdom
33rd Sunday in Ordinary Time
Readings: Prv 31:10–13, 19–20, 30–31;
1 Thes 5:1–6; Mt 25:14–30
Related Topics: Social Justice, Evil,
Forgiveness, Fear of the Lord
Christ the King
Readings: Ez 34:11–12, 15–17;
1 Cor 15:20–26, 28; Mt 25:31–46
Related Topics: Judgment, Kingdom,
Hospitality, Healing, Service
Assumption - August 15
Readings: Rv 11:19a, 12:1–6a, 10ab;
1 Cor 15:20–26; Lk 1:39–56
Related Topics: Mary, Eschatology,
Justice and Peace, Resurrection,
Assumption, Christian Hope, Pastoral
on the Economy, Jesus
Immaculate Conception - December 8
Readings: Gn 3:9–15, 20; Eph 1:3–6,
11–12; Lk 1:26–38
Related Topics: Theology of Grace,
Original Sin, Free Will, Role of Mary,
Distinction between the Immaculate
Conception and Virgin Birth,
Stewardship of Gifts, Social Sin,
Reconciliation

Feast of All Saints - November 1
Readings: Rv 7:2–3, 9–14; 1 Jn 3:1–3;
Mt 5:1–12a
Related Topics: Communion of Saints,
Intercession, Beatitudes, Holiness,
Justice, Care of the Poor,
Contemplation
Mary, Mother of God - Jan 1
Readings: Nm 6:22–27; Gal 4:4–7;
Lk 2:16–21
Related Topics: Marian Devotion; Mary,
Mother of God; Mary, Model of
Church; Peace; "Word"; Blessing;
Salvation; Liberation; Christology;
Jesus in Ordinary Life
Epiphany
Readings: Is 60:1–6; Eph 3:2–3, 5–6,
Mt 2:1–12
Related Topics: Christ as Light of
World, Universality of Church, U.S.
Bishops' Peace Pastoral, Epiphany,
Journey, Magi, Gift, Conversion,
Revelation, Inspiration, Prayer,
Constitution on Divine Revelation
Ash Wednesday
Readings: Jl 2:12–18; 2 Cor 5:20—6:2;
Mt 6:1–6, 16–18
Related Topics: Sin, Repentance,
Justification, Temptation, Lent,
Christian Witness, Liturgical Seasons,
Penance
Easter Sunday
Readings: Acts 10:34, 37–43;
Col 3:1–14 or 1 Cor 5:6–8, Jn 20:1–9
Related Topics: Resurrection, Easter,
Catholicity, Christian Initiation,
Revelation, Church, Incarnation,
Theological Virtues, Immanent and
Transcendent God, Absence and
Presence of God, Faith Experience,
Paschal Mystery, Belief, Celebration
and Traditions
Pentecost Sunday
Readings: Acts 2:1–11; 1 Cor 12:3–7,
12–13; Jn 20:19–23
Related Topics: Holy Spirit, Charisms,
Gifts and Fruits, Symbols, Church,
Mission, Ministry, Community,
Renewal in the Church, Authority in
the Church, Spirit's Work in the
Church, Forgiveness of Sins, Pentecost,
Peace

Cycle B

First Sunday of Advent
Readings: Is 63:16b–17, 19b, 64:2–7;
1 Cor 1:3–9; Mk 13:33–37
Related Topics: God's Initiative, God's
Faithfulness, Prayer-Thanksgiving,
Hope, Advent
Second Sunday of Advent
Readings: Is 40:1–5, 9–11; 2 Pt 3:8–14;
Mk 1:1–8
Related Topics: Justice—Corporal
Works of Mercy, Forgiveness,
Giftedness and Waiting, Patience
Third Sunday of Advent
Readings: Is 61:1–2a, 10–11;
1 Thes 5:16–24; Jn 1:6–8, 19–28
Related Topics: Prophet, Church,
Discerning Community, Conversion,
Justice and Peace, Hope
Fourth Sunday of Advent
Readings: 2 Sm 7:1–5, 8b–11, 16;
Rom 16:25–27; Lk 1:26–38
Related Topics: Trinity, Revelation,
Church—Discerning Community,
Mary—Model Disciple
Christmas (See Cycle A)
Holy Family
Readings: Sir 3:2–6, 12–14;
Col 3:12–21; Lk 2:22–40
Related Topics: Liturgy—Prayer of the
Church; Virtues—Forgiveness and Love;
Trinity; Family—Christian Family
Baptism of the Lord
Readings: Is 42:1–4, 6–7;
Acts 10:34–38; Mk 1:7–11
Related Topics: Trinity, Baptism,
Mission/Service, Power, Authority, Call
to Holiness, Sacrament of Initiation,
Pivotal Decision in Life and Faith
First Sunday of Lent
Readings: Gn 9:8–15; 1 Pt 3:18–22;
Mk 1:12–15
Related Topics: Fasting, Election,
Covenant, Baptism, Repentance, Lent
Second Sunday of Lent
Readings: Gn 22:1–2, 9, 10–13, 15–18;
Rom 8:31–34; Mk 9:2–10
Related Topics: Faith, Glory of God,
Transformation, Love, Religious
Experience, Service, Hope

Third Sunday of Lent
Readings: Ex 20:1–17; 1 Cor 1:22–25;
Jn 2:13–25
Related Topics: Covenant, Image of
Messiah, Paradox of Strength in
Weakness, Temple, Ten
Commandments, Law
Fourth Sunday of Lent
Readings: 2 Chr 36:14–16, 19–23;
Eph 2:4–10; Jn 3:14–21
Related Topics: Unconditional Love,
Salvation as a Free Gift, Cross as
Exaltation, Typology, Faith
Fifth Sunday of Lent
Readings: Jer 31:31–34; Heb 5:7–9;
Jn 12:20–33
Related Topics: Covenant,
Divinity/Humanity of Jesus,
Discipleship, Community, Ministry as
Sharing Food, Eucharist
Passion Sunday—Palm Sunday
Procession with Palms: Mk 11:1–10
Readings: Is 50:4–7; Phil 2:6–11;
Mk 15:1–39
Related Topics: Paschal Mystery,
Redemption, Salvation, Ultimate
Choice
Second Sunday of Easter
Readings: Acts 4:32–35; 1 Jn 5:1–6;
Jn 20:19–31
Related Topics: Forgiveness,
Reconciliation, Peace, Faith, Holy
Spirit, Doubt, Christian Community
Third Sunday of Easter
Readings: Acts 3:13–15, 17–19;
1 Jn 2:1–5; Lk 24:35–48
Related Topics: Death and Resurrection,
Sin, Mission and Witness, Trust and
Hope, Scriptures Fulfilled
Fourth Sunday of Easter
Readings: Acts 4:8–12; 1 Jn 3:1–2;
Jn 10:11–18
Related Topics: Images of God in
Scripture, Leadership, Universality of
Christ, Ecumenism, Good Shepherd
Fifth Sunday of Easter
Readings: Acts 9:26–31; 1 Jn 3:18–24;
Jn 15:1–8
Related Topics: Church, Leadership,
Body of Christ, Mission, Ministry,
Discipleship, Gifts, Sin, Petition,
Prayer, Simplicity

Sixth Sunday of Easter
Readings: Acts 10:25–26, 34–35,
44–48; 1 Jn 4:7–10; Jn 15:9–17
Related Topics: Theological Virtues,
Commandments, Death and
Resurrection of Christ, Martyrs and
Saints, Revelation, Mission and
Ministry, Call, Responding to God's
Love
Ascension
Readings: Acts 1:1–11; Eph 1:17–23;
Mk 16:15–20
Related Topics: Salvation,
Evangelization, Holy Spirit, Gifts,
Ascension, Afterlife
Seventh Sunday of Easter
Readings: Acts 1:15–17, 20–26;
1 Jn 4:11–16; Jn 17:11–19
Related Topics: World and Church
Relationship, Mission and Ministry,
Morality, Social Justice, Truth and
Wisdom, Guidance
Trinity Sunday
Readings: Dt 4:32–34, 39–40;
Rom 8:14–17; Mt 28:16–20
Related Topics: Trinity, Prayer of the
Church as Proclamation of Its
Teaching, Creed
Feast of Corpus Christi
Readings: Ex 24:3–8; Heb 9:11–15,
Mk 14:12–16, 22–26
Related Topics: Eucharist, Passover,
Passover Meal, Real Presence, Body of
Christ, Covenant
Second Sunday in Ordinary Time
Readings: 1 Sm 3:3–10, 19;
1 Cor 6:13–15, 17–20; Jn 1:35–42
Related Topics: Vocation, Sacraments,
Universal Call to Holiness, Discerning
the Lord's Call
Third Sunday in Ordinary Time
Readings: Jon 3:1–5, 10;
1 Cor 7:29–31; Mk 1:14–20
Related Topics: Sacrament of Marriage,
Universal Call to Holiness, Simple Life-
style, Conversion
Fourth Sunday in Ordinary Time
Readings: Dt 18:15–20; 1 Cor 7:32–35;
Mk 1:21–28
Related Topics: Sacrament of
Reconciliation, Spiritual Direction,
Conversion as an Ongoing Call,

Marriage and Celibacy, Vocation
Fifth Sunday in Ordinary Time
Readings: Jb 7:1–4, 6–7; 1 Cor
9:16–19, 22–23; Mk 1:29–39
Related Topics: Sacrament of
Anointing, Healing, Forgiveness,
Suffering, Problem of Evil
Sixth Sunday in Ordinary Time
Readings: Lv 13:1–2, 44–46;
1 Cor 10:31—11:1; Mk 1:40–45
Related Topics: Faith Development,
Stages of Growth, Creed, Presentation
of the Traditions, Unity and
Community
Seventh Sunday in Ordinary Time
Readings: Is 43:18–19, 21–22, 24–25;
2 Cor 1:18–22; Mk 2:1–12
Related Topics: Forgiveness, Miracles of
Healing, Christian Community
Eighth Sunday in Ordinary Time
Readings: Hos 2:16–17, 21–22;
2 Cor 3:1–6; Mk 2:18–22
Related Topics: New Covenant
Members, Living Gospel Values, Love,
Solitude, Holy Spirit
Ninth Sunday in Ordinary Time
Readings: Dt 5:12–15; 2 Cor 4:6–11;
Mk 2:23—3:6 (long form); or 2:23–28
(short form)
Related Topics: Keeping the Sabbath,
Time for Prayer, Commandments
Tenth Sunday in Ordinary Time
Readings: Gn 3:9–15; 2 Cor 4:13—5:1;
Mk 3:20–35
Related Topics: Promise of
Redemption, Basis Option, Spiritual
Growth, Journal Keeping, Personified
Evil
Eleventh Sunday in Ordinary Time
Readings: Ez 17:22–24; 2 Cor 5:6–10;
Mk 4:26–34
Related Topics: Christian Hope,
Salvation, Eschatology
Twelfth Sunday in Ordinary Time
Readings: Jb 38:1, 8–11;
2 Cor 5:14–17; Mk 4:35–41
Related Topics: Formation of Scripture,
History of the Gospels, Scripture in the
Liturgy, Trust in God, Miracles
Thirteenth Sunday in Ordinary Time
Readings: Wis 1:13–15, 2:23–24;
2 Cor 8:7–9, 13–15; Mk 5:21–43

Related Topics: Healing, Prejudice and Pride, Power of Jesus, Anointing of the Sick, Miracles, Reconciliation, Life

Fourteenth Sunday in Ordinary Time
Readings: Ez 2:2–5; 2 Cor 12:7–10; Mk 6:1–6
Related Topics: Divinity and Humanity of Christ, Discipleship, Pain of Rejection, Witness, Truth, Prophecy

Fifteenth Sunday in Ordinary Time
Readings: Am 7:12–15; Eph 1:3–14; Mk 6:7–13
Related Topics: Christian Call to Mission, Discipleship, Holy Orders, Ministry in the Church, Stewardship, Church and State

Sixteenth Sunday in Ordinary Time
Readings: Jer 23:1–6; Eph 2:13–18; Mk 6:30–34
Related Topics: Compassion of God, Love for Others, Christian Justice, Suffering, Church Leadership

Seventeenth Sunday in Ordinary Time
Readings: 2 Kgs 4:42–44; Eph 4:1–6; Jn 6:1–15
Related Topics: Eucharist, Social Justice, Responsibility to the Poor, World Hunger, Corporal Works of Mercy, Poverty

Eighteenth Sunday in Ordinary Time
Readings: Ex 16:2–4, 12–15; Eph 4:17, 20–24; Jn 6:24–35
Related Topics: Worship, Eucharist, Incarnation and Conversion, Economic Pastoral, Greed, False Gods

Nineteenth Sunday in Ordinary Time
Readings: 1 Kgs 9:4–8; Eph 4:30—5:2; Jn 6:41–51
Related Topics: Humanity and Divinity of Christ, Eucharistic Presence, Liturgy and Spirituality

20th Sunday in Ordinary Time
Readings: Prv 9:1–6; Eph 5:15–20; Jn 6:51–58
Related Topics: Eucharist, Prayer, Ecumenism, Wisdom

21st Sunday in Ordinary Time
Readings: Jos 24:1–2, 15–17, 18; Eph 5:21–32; Jn 6:60–69
Related Topics: Dogma, Eucharist, Relationship with the Lord, Moral Decision Making, Discipleship

22nd Sunday in Ordinary Time
Readings: Dt 4:1–2, 6–8; Jas 1:17–18, 21–22, 27; Mk 7:1–8, 14–15, 21–23
Related Topics: Christian Growth, Spirituality, Church Laws, Religious Practices, Rites and Rituals, Church Authority, Dissent, Tradition, Discipleship

23rd Sunday in Ordinary Time
Readings: Is 35:4–7; Jas 2:1–5; Mk 7:31–37
Related Topics: Healing, Prejudice, Miracles, Compassion to the Handicapped, Discipleship, Revelation, Scriptures

24th Sunday in Ordinary Time
Readings: Is 50:4–9; Jas 2:14–18; Mk 8:27–35
Related Topics: Christology, Suffering Servant, Paschal Mystery, Faith and Good Works, Death and Dying, Discipleship

25th Sunday in Ordinary Time
Readings: Wis 2:12, 17–20; Jas 3:16–4:3; Mk 9:30–37
Related Topics: Stewardship, Ministry, Leadership, Death and Fear of Death, Christian Values

26th Sunday in Ordinary Time
Readings: Nm 11:25–29; Jas 5:1–6, Mk 9:38–43, 45, 47–48
Related Topics: Ecumenism, Social Justice, Materialism, Pastoral on the Economy, Afterlife, Heaven and Hell, Eschatology, Money and the Kingdom

27th Sunday in Ordinary Time
Readings: Gn 2:18–24; Heb 2:9–11; Mk 10:2–16
Related Topics: Theology of Marriage, Christian and Jewish Perspectives on Marriage, Divorce and Annulments, Process of Death and Dying, Separations and Endings, Human Dignity

28th Sunday in Ordinary Time
Readings: Wis 7:7–11; Heb 4:12–13; Mk 10:17–30
Related Topics: Materialism, Social Justice, Stewardship, Illness and Healing, Presence of God

29th Sunday in Ordinary Time
Readings: Is 53:10–11; Heb 4:14–16; Mk 10:35–45

Related Topics: Church Hierarchy, Ministry of the Faithful, Servant Leadership, Humanity of Christ

30th Sunday in Ordinary Time
Readings: Jer 31:7–9; Heb 5:1–6; Mk 10:46–52
Related Topics: The Priesthood of Jesus, Healing, New Testament Miracles, Pastoral Care of the Sick, Communion of Saints, Christian Burial, Thirsting for God

31st Sunday in Ordinary Time
Readings: Dt 6:2–6; Heb 7:23–28; Mk 12:28–34
Related Topics: Hebrew and Christian Covenants, Social Justice Issues, Pastoral on the Economy, Funeral Rite, Love

32nd Sunday in Ordinary Time
Readings: 1 Kgs 17:10–16; Heb 9:24–28; Mk 12:38–44
Related Topics: Scripture Images of Priesthood, Christmas, Stewardship, Economics, Social Justice, Trust God

33rd Sunday in Ordinary Time
Readings: Dn 12:1–3; Heb 10:11–14, 18; Mk 13:24–32
Related Topics: Eschatology, Day of Judgment, Apocalyptic Literature, Gospel of Mark

Christ the King
Readings: Dn 7:13–14; Rev 1:5–8; Jn 18:33–37
Related Topics: Christology, Apocalyptic Literature, Advent, God's Reign, Day of Judgment, Kingdom

Assumption - August 15
Readings: Rv 11:19a, 12:1–6a, 10ab; 1 Cor 15:20–26; Lk 1:39–56
Related Topics: Mary, Eschatology, Justice and Peace, Resurrection, Assumption, Christian Hope, Pastoral on the Economy, Jesus

Immaculate Conception - December 8
Readings: Gn 3:9–15, 20; Eph 1:3–6, 11–12; Lk 1:26–38
Related Topics: Theology of Grace, Original Sin, Free Will, Role of Mary, Distinction between the Immaculate Conception and Virgin Birth, Stewardship of Gifts, Social Sin, Reconciliation

Feast of All Saints - November 1
Readings: Rv 7:2–3, 9–14; 1 Jn 3:1–3; Mt 5:1–12a
Related Topics: Communion of Saints, Intercession, Beatitudes, Holiness, Justice, Care of the Poor, Contemplation

Mary, Mother of God - Jan 1
Readings: Nm 6:22–27; Gal 4:4–7; Lk 2:16–21
Related Topics: Marian Devotion; Mary, Mother of God; Mary, Model of Church; Peace; "Word"; Blessing; Salvation; Liberation; Christology; Jesus in Ordinary Life

Epiphany
Readings: Is 60:1–6; Eph 3:2–3, 5–6, Mt 2:1–12
Related Topics: Christ as Light of World, Universality of Church, U.S. Bishops' Peace Pastoral, Epiphany, Journey, Magi, Gift, Conversion, Revelation, Inspiration, Prayer, Constitution on Divine Revelation

Ash Wednesday
Readings: Jl 2:12–18; 2 Cor 5:20–6:2; Mt 6:1–6, 16–18
Related Topics: Sin, Repentance, Justification, Temptation, Lent, Christian Witness, Liturgical Seasons, Penance

Easter Sunday
Readings: Acts 10:34, 37–43; Col 3:1–14 or 1 Cor 5:6–8; Jn 20:1–9
Related Topics: Resurrection, Easter, Catholicity, Christian Initiation, Revelation, Church, Incarnation, Theological Virtues, Immanent and Transcendent God, Absence and Presence of God, Faith Experience, Paschal Mystery, Belief, Celebration and Traditions

Pentecost Sunday
Readings: Acts 2:1–11; 1 Cor 12:3–7, 12–13; Jn 20:19–23
Related Topics: Holy Spirit, Charisms, Gifts and Fruits, Symbols, Church, Mission, Ministry, Community, Renewal in the Church, Authority in the Church, Spirit's Work in the Church, Forgiveness of Sins, Pentecost, Peace

Cycle C

First Sunday of Advent
Readings: Jer 33:14–16;
1 Thes 3:12–4:2; Lk 21:25–28, 34–36
Related Topics: Advent, Conversion,
Transformation, Eschatology, Death-
Resurrection, Suffering, Jesus
Second Sunday of Advent
Readings: Bar 5:1–9; Phil 1:4–6, 8–11;
Lk 3:1–6
Related Topics: Repentance, Sacrament
of Reconciliation, Healing, Conversion,
Forgiveness, Humility, Eschatology
Third Sunday of Advent
Readings: Zep 3:14–18; Phil 4:4–7;
Lk 3:10–18
Related Topics: Conversion, Grace,
Surrender, Justice, Baptism, Judgment,
Christian Living, Prayer, Peace, Jesus
Fourth Sunday of Advent
Readings: Mi 5:1–4; Heb 10:5–10;
Lk 1:39–45
Related Topics: Mary, Incarnation,
Peace, Salvation, Jesus
Christmas (See Cycle A)
Holy Family Sunday
Readings: Sir 3:2–6, 12–14;
Col 3:12–21; Lk 2:41–52
Related Topics: Christian Family,
Parenting, Christian Love, Fourth
Commandment, Marriage, Liturgy,
Peace
Baptism of the Lord
Readings: Is 42:1–4, 6–7;
Acts 10:34–38; Lk 3:15–16, 21–22
Related Topics: Baptism, Ministry, Faith
and Doubt, Holy Spirit, Christian
Unity, Salvation, Social Justice, Peace
First Sunday of Lent
Readings: Dt 26:4–10; Rom 10:8–13;
Lk 4:1–13
Related Topics: Temptation, Salvation
History, Conversion, Lenten Customs,
Wisdom, Moral Issues
Second Sunday of Lent
Readings: Gn 15:5–12, 17–18;
Phil 3:17—4:1; Lk 9:28–36
Related Topics: Transfiguration,
Transformation, Journey of Salvation,
Prophets, Spiritual Journey,
Righteousness and Faith

Third Sunday of Lent
Readings: Ex 3:1–8, 13–15;
1 Cor 10:1–6, 10–12; Lk 13:1–9
Related Topics: Repentance, Social
Justice, Prayer, God's Presence,
Religious Experience
Fourth Sunday of Lent
Readings: Jos 5:9, 10–12;
2 Cor 5:17–21; Lk 15:1–3, 11–32
Related Topics: Forgiveness, Mercy,
Justice, Rites of Penance, Yearning for
More, Reconciliation
Fifth Sunday of Lent
Readings: Is 43:16–21; Phil 3:8–14;
Jn 8:1–11
Related Topics: Redemption, Self-
Awareness, Holiness, Faith
Development, Judging Others
Passion Sunday—Palm Sunday
Readings: Procession with Palms:
Lk 19:28–40; Is 50:4–7; Phil 2:6–11;
Lk 23:1–49
Related Topics: Images of God,
Sacramentals, Death and Resurrection,
Holy Week
Second Sunday of Easter
Readings: Acts 5:12–16; Rev 1:9–11,
12–13, 17–19; Jn 20:19–31
Related Topics: Belief and Doubt,
History of Creeds, Paschal Mystery,
Church, Miracles and Visions
Third Sunday of Easter
Readings: Acts 5:27–32, 40–41;
Rv 5:11–14; Jn 21:1–19
Related Topics: Vocation, Pastoral on
Peace, Pastoral on Economy, Social
Justice, Resurrection
Fourth Sunday of Easter
Readings: Acts 13:14, 43–52; Rev 7:9,
14–17; Jn 10:27–30
Related Topics: Hierarchy, Pastoral
Leadership, Catholic Worker Houses,
Image of God, Trust, Good Shepherd
Fifth Sunday of Easter
Readings: Acts 14:21–27; Rev 21:1–5;
Jn 13:31–33, 34–35
Related Topics: Theological Virtues,
Parish Life, Social Justice, Conviction,
Commitment, Love
Sixth Sunday of Easter
Readings: Acts 15:1–2, 22–29;
Rv 21:10–14, 22–23; Jn 14:23–29

Related Topics: Prayer, Conscience, Heaven, Discernment, Fear, Peace

Ascension Thursday
Readings: Acts 1:1–11; Eph 1:17–23; Lk 24:46–53
Related Topics: Models of the Church, Body of Christ, Liturgical Prayer, Power, Authority, Kingdom of God

Seventh Sunday of Easter
Readings: Acts 7:55–60; Rev 22:12–14, 16–17, 20; Jn 17:20–26
Related Topics: Ecumenism, Second Vatican Council, Signs of the Church, Diaconate and Ministry, Unity, Forgiveness

Trinity Sunday
Readings: Prv 8:22–31; Rom 5:1–5; Jn 16:12–15
Related Topics: Trinity; Creed; Inclusive Language; Theological Virtues of Faith, Hope, and Love; God's Presence

Feast of Corpus Christi
Readings: Gn 14:18–20; 1 Cor 11:23–26; Lk 9:11–17
Related Topics: Eucharist, Sacrament, Social Justice and the Hungry, Kingdom, Anointing, Body of Christ

Second Sunday in Ordinary Time
Readings: Is 62:1–5; 1 Cor 12:4–11; Jn 2:1–12
Related Topics: Signs, Sacraments, Covenant, Church as Sacrament, Miracles, Jesus, Mary, Gifts of the Spirit

Third Sunday in Ordinary Time
Readings: Neh 8:2–4, 5–6, 8–10; 1 Cor 12:12–30; Lk 1:1–4; 4:14–21
Related Topics: Power of the Spirit, Jesus, Mission, Isaiah, Prophet, Law, Teacher, Economic Pastoral

Fourth Sunday in Ordinary Time
Readings: Jer 1:4–5, 17–19; 1 Cor 12:31—13:13; Lk 4:21–30
Related Topics: Charity, Corinthians, Paul, Prophets, Prophecy, Rejection, Mission, Hebrew Scriptures, Elijah, Elisha, Naaman, Universal Mission

Fifth Sunday in Ordinary Time
Readings: Is 6:1–2, 3–8; 1 Cor 15:1–11; Lk 5:1–11
Related Topics: Call, Vocation, Discipleship, Ministry, Simon Peter, Apostles, Storytelling, Holiness

Sixth Sunday in Ordinary Time
Readings: Jer 17:5–8; 1 Cor 15:12, 16–20; Lk 6:17, 20–26
Related Topics: Beatitudes, Disciples, Justice, Witness, Conversion, Reign of God, Hope

Seventh Sunday in Ordinary Time
Readings: 1 Sm 26:2, 7–9, 12–13, 22–23; 1 Cor 15:45–49; Lk 6:27–38
Related Topics: Living the Beatitudes, Witness, Compassion, Life-style, Love of Enemies, Parables, Justice, Charity, Magnanimity

Eighth Sunday in Ordinary Time
Readings: Sir 27:4–7; 1 Cor 15:54–58; Lk 6:39–45
Related Topics: Word, Motivation, Evil, Jesus as Teacher, Judging, Conversion, Discernment, Practicalities

Ninth Sunday in Ordinary Time
Readings: 1 Kgs 8:41–43; Gal 1:1–2, 6–10; Lk 7:1–10
Related Topics: Faith, Healing, Miracles, Jesus' Healing Ministry, Obedience

Tenth Sunday in Ordinary Time
Readings: 1 Kgs 17:17–24; Gal 1:11–19; Lk 7:11–17
Related Topics: Compassion, Widows, Elisha, Miracle, Resurrection, Death, Sources

Eleventh Sunday in Ordinary Time
Readings: 2 Sm 12:7–10, 13; Gal 2:16, 19–21; Lk 7:36—8:3
Related Topics: Parable, Pharisees, Forgiveness, Reconciliation, Sinners, Kingdom of God, Sexism, Women in Ministry

Twelfth Sunday in Ordinary Time
Readings: Zec 12:10–11; Gal 3:26–29; Lk 9:18–24
Related Topics: Cost of Discipleship, Christology, Jesus' Identity, Peter, Suffering, Cross, Prayer

Thirteenth Sunday in Ordinary Time
Readings: 1 Kgs 19:16, 19–21; Gal 5:1, 13–18; Lk 9:51–62
Related Topics: Church, Christian Life, Hospitality, Christian Freedom

Fourteenth Sunday in Ordinary Time
Readings: Is 66:10–14; Gal 6:14–18; Lk 10:1–12, 17–20

Related Topics: Baptism, Mission, Theological Virtues, Charisms, Authority and Power, Discipleship, Peace, Evangelization

Fifteenth Sunday in Ordinary Time
Readings: Dt 30:10–14; Col 1:15–20; Lk 10:25–37
Related Topics: Sacrament of Anointing, Sacrament of Reconciliation, Church Law, Hope, Paschal Mystery, Charity, Social Justice, Church and Politics, Simplicity

Sixteenth Sunday in Ordinary Time
Readings: Gn 18:1–10; Col 1:24–28; Lk 10:38–42
Related Topics: Catholic Prayer Forms, Christology, Contemporary Understanding of Prayer and Action

Seventeenth Sunday in Ordinary Time
Readings: Gn 18:20–32; Col 2:12–14; Lk 11:1–13
Related Topics: Kingdom of God; Reconciliation; Prayer; Eucharist; Petitionary Prayer; Perseverance; Prayers in Scripture; Prayer Forms; Faith, Hope, and Love; Divine Revelation

Eighteenth Sunday in Ordinary Time
Readings: Eccl 1:2, 2:21–23; Col 3:1–5, 9–11; Lk 12:13–21
Related Topics: Economy, Ecology (Sharing Earth's Goods), Saints, Stewardship, Giftedness of Creation (in O.T.)

Nineteenth Sunday in Ordinary Time
Readings: Wis 18:6–9; Heb 11:1–2, 8–19; Lk 12:32–48
Related Topics: Kingdom, Heaven, Eucharist, Eschatology, Salvation, Social Justice, Theological Virtues, Fear

20th Sunday in Ordinary Time
Readings: Jer 38:4–6, 8–10; Heb 12:1–4; Lk 12:49–53
Related Topics: Social Justice, Prophecy, Prophets, Kingdom, Paschal Mystery, Early Christian Community, Martyrs, Redemption, Cost of Discipleship

21st Sunday in Ordinary Time
Readings: Is 66:18–21; Heb 12:5–7, 11–13; Lk 13:22–30
Related Topics: Conversion, Ecumenism, Salvation, Kingdom of

God, Hope, Faith, Heaven and Hell

22nd Sunday in Ordinary Time
Readings: Sir 3:17–18, 20, 28–29; Heb 12:18–19, 22–24; Lk 14:1, 7–14
Related Topics: Fruits of the Spirit, Eucharist, Church Law, Authority, Ecclesiology, Social Justice, Ministry and Mission of the Church, Divorce and Remarriage, Healing, Sacrament of Reconciliation, Humility

23rd Sunday in Ordinary Time
Readings: Wis 9:13–18; Phlm 9–10, 12–17; Lk 14:25–33
Related Topics: Discipleship, Mission of the Church, Ministry, Evangelization, Judgment, Sin, Conversion, Trinity, God, Mystery, Revelation, Stewardship

24th Sunday in Ordinary Time
Readings: Ex 32:7–11, 13–14; 1 Tm 1:12–17; Lk 15:1–32
Related Topics: Mercy, Faithfulness, Forgiveness, Celebration, Reconciliation

25th Sunday in Ordinary Time
Readings: Am 8:4–7; 1 Tm 2:1–8; Lk 16:1–13
Related Topics: Justice, Economic Pastoral, Stewardship, Authority and Power, Social Sin, Social Consciousness

26th Sunday in Ordinary Time
Readings: Am 6:1, 4–7; 1 Tm 6:11–16; Lk 16:19–31
Related Topics: Christian Life-style, Justice, Body of Christ, Stewardship, Humility, Faith

27th Sunday in Ordinary Time
Readings: Heb 1:2–3, 2:2–4; 2 Tm 1:6–8, 13–14; Lk 17:5–10
Related Topics: Faith, Doubt, Salvation, Thanksgiving, Eucharist, God's Healing, Creed

28th Sunday in Ordinary Time
Readings: 2 Kgs 5:14–17; 2 Tm 2:8–13; Lk 17:11–19
Related Topics: Salvation, Healing, Faith, Power of God, Prejudice, Dying and Rising with Christ

29th Sunday in Ordinary Time
Readings: Ex 17:8–13; 2 Tm 3:14—4:2; Lk 18:1–8
Related Topics: Justice, Christian

Action, Prayer, Revelation, Intercession
30th Sunday in Ordinary Time
Readings: Sir 35:12–14, 16–18;
2 Tm 4:6–8, 16–18; Lk 18:9–14
Related Topics: Patience, Prayer,
Humility, Faith, Sacrifice, Self-Gift,
Pharisees, Salvation, Eucharist,
Problem of Evil
31st Sunday in Ordinary Time
Readings: Wis 11:22—12:1;
2 Thes 1:11—2:2; Lk 19:1–10
Related Topics: Real Presence, Sin,
Repentance, Call, Justice, Beatitudes,
Eschatology
32nd Sunday in Ordinary Time
Readings: 2 Mc 7:1–2, 9–14;
2 Thes 2:16—3:5; Lk 20:27–38
Related Topics: Death, Heaven, Hell,
Resurrection, Afterlife, Hope,
Communion of Saints, Holiness and
Sanctity
33rd Sunday in Ordinary Time
Readings: Mal 3:19–20; 2 Thes 3:7–12;
Lk 21:5–19
Related Topics: Service, Eschatology,
Hope, Kingdom of God, Persecution,
Cost of Discipleship
Christ the King
Readings: 2 Sm 5:1–3; Col 1:12–20;
Lk 23:35–43
Related Topics: Christ the King,
Kingdom of God, Power, Authority,
Leadership, Justice, Stewards of
Creation
Assumption - August 15
Readings: Rv 11:19a, 12:1–6a, 10ab;
1 Cor 15:20–26; Lk 1:39–56
Related Topics: Mary, Eschatology,
Justice and Peace, Resurrection,
Assumption, Christian Hope, Pastoral
on the Economy, Jesus
Immaculate Conception - December 8
Readings: Gn 3:9–15, 20; Eph 1:3–6,
11–12; Lk 1:26–38
Related Topics: Theology of Grace,
Original Sin, Free Will, Role of Mary,
Distinction between the Immaculate
Conception and Virgin Birth,
Stewardship of Gifts, Social Sin,
Reconciliation

Feast of All Saints - November 1
Readings: Rv 7:2–3, 9–14; 1 Jn 3:1–3;
Mt 5:1–12a
Related Topics: Communion of Saints,
Intercession, Beatitudes, Holiness,
Justice, Care of the Poor, Contemplation
Mary, Mother of God - Jan 1
Readings: Nm 6:22–27; Gal 4:4–7;
Lk 2:16–21
Related Topics: Marian Devotion; Mary,
Mother of God; Mary, Model of
Church; Peace; "Word"; Blessing;
Salvation; Liberation; Christology;
Jesus in Ordinary Life
Epiphany
Readings: Is 60:1–6; Eph 3:2–3, 5–6,
Mt 2:1–12
Related Topics: Christ as Light of
World, Universality of Church, U.S.
Bishops' Peace Pastoral, Epiphany,
Journey, Magi, Gift, Conversion,
Revelation, Inspiration, Prayer,
Constitution on Divine Revelation
Ash Wednesday
Readings: Jl 2:12–18; 2 Cor 5:20–6:2;
Mt 6:1–6, 16–18
Related Topics: Sin, Repentance,
Justification, Temptation, Lent, Christian
Witness, Liturgical Seasons, Penance
Easter Sunday
Readings: Acts 10:34, 37–43;
Col 3:1–14 or 1 Cor 5:6–8, Jn 20:1–9
Related Topics: Resurrection, Easter,
Catholicity, Christian Initiation,
Revelation, Church, Incarnation,
Theological Virtues, Immanent and
Transcendent God, Absence and
Presence of God, Faith Experience,
Paschal Mystery, Belief, Celebration
and Traditions
Pentecost Sunday
Readings: Acts 2:1–11; 1 Cor 12:3–7,
12–13; Jn 20:19–23
Related Topics: Holy Spirit, Charisms,
Gifts and Fruits, Symbols, Church,
Mission, Ministry, Community,
Renewal in the Church, Authority in
the Church, Spirit's work in the
Church, Forgiveness of Sins, Pentecost,
Peace